ASKING FOR IT

ASKING FOR IT

and

WHAT I CALL HER

two plays by

Ellie Moon

with a Foreword by Martha Schabas

Talonbooks

© 2020 Ellie Moon
Foreword © 2020 Martha Schabas

All rights reserved. No part of this book may be reproduced, stored in a retrieval system, or transmitted, in any form or by any means, without the prior written consent of the publisher or a licence from Access Copyright (The Canadian Copyright Licensing Agency). For a copyright licence, visit accesscopyright.ca or call toll-free 1-800-893-5777.

Talonbooks
9259 Shaughnessy Street, Vancouver, British Columbia, Canada V6P 6R4
talonbooks.com

Talonbooks is located on xʷməθkʷəy̓əm, Sḵwx̱wú7mesh, and səl̓ilwətaʔɬ Lands.

First printing: 2020

Typeset in Minion
Printed and bound in Canada on 100% post-consumer recycled paper

Interior design by andrea bennett, cover design by Chloë Filson
Cover illustration by Thom Nyhuus

Talonbooks acknowledges the financial support of the Canada Council for the Arts, the Government of Canada through the Canada Book Fund, and the Province of British Columbia through the British Columbia Arts Council and the Book Publishing Tax Credit.

Rights to produce *Asking for It and What I Call Her*, in whole or in part, in any medium by any group, amateur or professional, are retained by the author. Interested persons are requested to contact Colin Rivers at Marquis Entertainment: 73 Richmond Street West, #312, Toronto, Ontario, M5H 4E8; 416-960-9123; crivers@marquisent.ca; mqent.ca.

LIBRARY AND ARCHIVES CANADA CATALOGUING IN PUBLICATION

Title: Asking for it : and What I call her / Ellie Moon ; with an introduction by Martha Schabas.
Other titles: Plays. Selections | What I call her
Names: Moon, Ellie, 1993– author. | Schabas, Martha, writer of introduction. | Container of (work): Moon, Ellie, 1993– Asking for it. | Container of (work): Moon, Ellie, 1993– What I call her.
Identifiers: Canadiana 20200261789 | ISBN 9781772012668 (SOFTCOVER)
Classification: LCC PS8626.O592635 A6 2020 | DDC C812/.6—dc23

Thoughts are often false. A feeling's always real. Not true, just real.

—Susan Choi, *Trust Exercise* (2019)

CONTENTS

Foreword by Martha Schabas　ix

Asking for It　1

What I Call Her　101

Acknowledgments　211

FOREWORD

BY MARTHA SCHABAS

Asking for It opened in Toronto in early October of 2017, days after the first rape and sexual assault allegations were made against Hollywood producer Harvey Weinstein, and just as the term #MeToo was beginning to trend online. To call the play timely seems a considerable understatement – at least, that's how I pitched it to my *Globe and Mail* editor when I suggested that I attend opening night and write a related think piece on sex and consent. But things didn't go as I'd planned at the theatre – an experience I've since come to expect of Ellie Moon's creations. The play got under my skin in a way that was uncomfortable for me to think about, let alone parse publicly, and I grappled with my responsibilities to my readers and employer versus my desire to cancel the article and just tune out.

There's something feral about Moon's writing. I felt it that first night at Crow's Theatre, watching everyday depictions of seduction and coercion, of characters avowing certain beliefs and then immediately acting against them, of discussions that were simultaneously unsettling and banal. The verbatim play – a series of recreated and reformatted interviews and conversations from Moon's life – was inspired by her interest in the topic of consent following CBC personality Jian Ghomeshi's highly publicized sexual assault trial. The scenarios it recreates aren't novel or sensational; Moon isn't interested in shocking her audience with salacious details or narrative twists. Instead, her theatre is discomfiting because it zooms in closer and closer to its subject until we can't look at the whole thing at once – she deprives us of the default contexts we normally rely on for understanding. Her theatre is relentless in the way that reality is relentless – it doesn't stop when we've had enough.

Seeing *What I Call Her*, the second play in this collection and a work of original content (i.e., not verbatim theatre), I felt this relentlessness even more. The play is about two estranged sisters and their contradictory feelings regarding their mother's terminal illness – the older sister claims the mother is a monster who physically abused her; the younger sister thinks this is a cruel and histrionic lie. The play could be called a she-said-she-said on conflicting childhood narratives, even a dialectic on the absolute subjectivity of truth. What makes it remarkable is how unflinchingly Moon pursues each psychological bias so that we are drawn into the pain of both perspectives and feel the burning indignation that comes with not having your story believed.

Moon is a playwright who likes words. Her characters are voluble, articulate, intelligent – they express themselves in unrestrained torrents of thought. These days, the term "naturalism" is often associated with a mumblecore aesthetic or inessential chitchat. Moon's naturalism is of a different order; her young women are politically engaged and restive, trying to balance their private turmoil with a world fraught with contentious contradictions. There's a recurring theme of going too far in Moon's plays – of letting the discord between the personal and political push these women beyond the brink of what's sane. It's a theme ready-made for diverse feminist analysis, particularly in what it suggests about the relationship between emotion and power. In Moon's world, power is always under scrutiny.

Moon's "too-muchness" is one of the principal joys of her writing, so give yourself over to it. Her dialogue explodes with an intellectual energy and psychological acuity rarely seen on Canadian stages. The plays in this collection are full of rewarding complexities; they're the work of a smart and irreverent artist whose career is just taking off.

These plays includes stories featuring emotional and violent experiences.

Audience and reader discretion are advised.

ASKING FOR IT

PRODUCTION HISTORY

Asking for It was first produced from October 6 to 21, 2017, by In Association with Crow's Theatre, Nightwood Theatre, and Necessary Angel in Toronto, Ontario, with the following cast and crew:

ELLIE	Ellie Moon
SECOND ACTOR, JIMMY, RADIO HOST, RICHARD, MITCH, BEN, NEW BRUNSWICK WOMAN, TYLER, SUBWAY MAN	Steven McCarthy
THIRD ACTOR, MARIA, WOMAN, HOPE, SOPHIE, DANA, NEW BRUNSWICK WOMAN, MARTHA SHAFFER, JOSIE, ADINA	Christine Horne
FOURTH ACTOR, HAT MAN, WILLIAM, NEW BRUNSWICK WOMAN, YAO, BRAD, PETER	Jaa Smith-Johnson

Director	Brendan Healy
Music and Sound Designer	Richard Feren
Lighting Designer	André du Toit
Stage Manager	Jordana Weiss
Producer	Geneviève Trottier

CHARACTERS

ELLIE, age twenty-two
SECOND ACTOR
THIRD ACTOR
FOURTH ACTOR
HAT MAN, in his thirties
MARIA, age twenty-two
JIMMY, in his fifties
RADIO HOST
WOMAN
HOPE, age sixteen, ELLIE and ADINA's sister
RICHARD, age sixty, ELLIE and HOPE's dad
SOPHIE, age twenty-three
WILLIAM
BEN
DANA, in her late thirties
MITCH
JOSIE
MARTHA SHAFFER, professor of criminal law
RADIO VOICE, a voice recording
NEW BRUNSWICK WOMAN
TYLER, age twenty-seven, police officer
YAO, in his late twenties
ADINA, age twelve, ELLIE and HOPE's sister
BRAD
SUBWAY MAN, in his late twenties
PETER, age twenty-four

PRODUCTION NOTES

Actors play multiple roles with the exception of the actor playing ELLIE, who should play her alone (but does voice some of the lines for NEW BRUNSWICK WOMAN in scene 13, as indicated).

The play's various settings should be indicated using lighting and sound. Minimal set and costumes are suggested.

A beat maintains the rhythm and shouldn't be held for too long. A silence is longer than a beat and can end at the actors' discretion.

ACT 1

TOP: Ellie Moon, Geoffrey Armour, and Michael Chiem in *Asking for It* at the Thousand Islands Playhouse, Gananoque, Ontario (September 13 to 29, 2019).
Photo by Randy deKleine-Stimpson. Reproduced with permission.

BOTTOM: Michael Chiem and Ellie Moon in *Asking for It* at the Thousand Islands Playhouse, Gananoque, Ontario (September 13 to 29, 2019).
Photo by Randy deKleine-Stimpson. Reproduced with permission.

SCENE 1

> *Lights up. All four actors take their places onstage.*

ELLIE
6:11 p.m., October 26, 2014.

SECOND ACTOR
(*quoting from or reading Jian Ghomeshi's Facebook post*)
"Dear everyone, I am writing today because I want you to be the first to know some news..."

THIRD ACTOR
"Today I was fired from the company where I've been working for almost fourteen years – stripped from my show, barred from the building, and separated from my colleagues."

FOURTH ACTOR
"I was given the choice to walk away quietly and to publicly suggest that this was my decision. But I am not going to do that."

ELLIE
"Because that would be untrue. Because I've been fired. And because I've done nothing wrong..."

SECOND ACTOR
"I have always been interested in a variety of activities in the bedroom, but I only participate in sexual practices that are mutually agreed upon, consensual, and exciting for both partners... Let me be the first to say that my tastes in the bedroom may not be palatable to some folks."

THIRD ACTOR
"They may be strange, enticing, weird, normal, or outright offensive to others. We all have our secret life. But that is my private life. That is my personal life. And no one, and certainly no employer, should have dominion over what people do consensually in their private life…"

FOURTH ACTOR
"I have lost my job based on a campaign of vengeance… I am still in shock. But I am telling this story to you so the truth is heard. And to bring an end to the nightmare."

ELLIE
102,009 people like this. Linda Reid McSpadden.

FOURTH ACTOR
"Disappointed… I thought a person was innocent until proven guilty…"

ELLIE
Elizabeth May.

SECOND ACTOR
"I think Jian is wonderful. Likely TMI for an old fogey like me, but his private life is none of our beeswax."

ELLIE
Joseph Michael Blank.

FOURTH ACTOR
"Kinky guy, crossed the line with a few women, probably should've opened a better dialogue with them first. That's it, that's all."

ELLIE
Robin Moore.

SECOND ACTOR
"For years he's supported a left-wing, pro-feminist, politically correct institution. He chose bedfellows politically, socially, and sexually… and now he's the one being fucked."

ELLIE
Lights.

THIRD ACTOR
"In my twelve years of working with and knowing Jian Ghomeshi, he has not only been a brilliant manager to my career, but a creative confidant, wise advisor, and dear friend. A complete gentleman. Jian is not an example of someone who is abusive or misogynistic, in fact, he has always preached the empowerment and limitless strength of women to me. I am angry that some are so quick to judge someone so graceful and brilliant who has made such an impact. I love you, Jian. You're my superhero."

ELLIE
In the space of four hours, Jian's "likes" drop to 3,689. Elizabeth May.

SECOND ACTOR
"So I guess one thing I've learned from this incident is: don't reply to tweets, don't stay on, don't stay engaged on Twitter when you know that you're feeling kind of emotional."

ELLIE
Lights.

THIRD ACTOR
"I posted comments about Jian Ghomeshi the day after he was dismissed by the CBC where I rushed to defend my manager of twelve years. I am now aware that my comments appear insensitive to those impacted, and for that I am

deeply sorry. This is to confirm that as of now I will be parting ways with Jian Ghomeshi as my manager."

ELLIE
Owen Pallett.

SECOND ACTOR
"Jian is my friend. I have appeared twice on Q. But there is no grey area here. Three women have been beaten by Jian Ghomeshi. I have sat with Jian over drinks and discussed our respective anxiety disorders. We have been photographed hugging on camera. Jian Ghomeshi is my friend, and Jian Ghomeshi beats women. How our friendship will continue remains to be seen."

SCENE 2

>*ELLIE waits at a light on the sidewalk. HAT MAN, wearing a hat that says "WATEVA," appears beside her. ELLIE admires his hat. They make eye contact.*

ELLIE
I like your hat.

HAT MAN
Thanks. How are you, darling?

ELLIE
I'm well, thanks. Yourself?

HAT MAN
Good.

>*Light changes. ELLIE and HAT MAN start walking.*

ELLIE
Have a good day, eh.

HAT MAN
Can I walk with you?

ELLIE
Um, sure, I'm in a bit of a hurry. Just on a lunch hour.

HAT MAN
You working?

ELLIE
Kind of. Rehearsing a play.

HAT MAN
Are you an actor?

ELLIE
Yes.

HAT MAN
Do you like that?

ELLIE
I love it.

HAT MAN
That's great. Hang on to that feeling.

ELLIE
Yeah, I will, thanks. What do you do?

HAT MAN
I'm in security. But studying accounting.

ELLIE
So you can beat people up, then take their money?

Beat.

Well, this is where I am.

HAT MAN
Is this where you're doing the play?

ELLIE
Yeah, it opens Friday – you should come.

HAT MAN
Cool. Can I have your number?

ELLIE
I'm sorry, I'm actually in a relationship.

HAT MAN
Really?

ELLIE
Yeah.

HAT MAN
Really.

ELLIE
Yeah. Is that so hard to believe...? Ha ha.

HAT MAN
Can I still have your number?

ELLIE
No.

HAT MAN
Why did you let me walk with you?

ELLIE
You asked.

HAT MAN
Why did you say you like my hat?

ELLIE
Because... I do. I'm sorry. I thought I was just being Canadian, friendly. I'm so sorry.

HAT MAN
Whatever.

ELLIE
(*to the audience*) Hi everyone, my name is Ellie. Thanks for being here tonight. Coming up to two years ago, I moved back to Canada after four years living in England. I was excited to reconnect with old friends and excited to start making eye contact with strangers again. I was in England at university when Ghomeshi-gate broke. No one around me there knew who Ghomeshi was, but I was closely following it on Facebook, and I wanted to talk about it, so I started bringing it up with British people. And some really incredible conversations came of that, and they didn't even know who Jian was. My friends there liked being invited to talk about experiences they felt not in control of, or in control of. I came back to Canada a year later, and started seeing old friends, and still wanted to talk. I put out a Facebook request for interview subjects, anyone who was willing to talk on record about Ghomeshi and sex, to make this play you're at tonight. Everyone you'll hear from has consented to be in the play, many on the condition that I protect their anonymity. So, I've done that, but will still try to give context where I can. Yeah, let's do it.

SCENE 3

ELLIE is having dinner at her apartment with MARIA.

ELLIE
(*to the audience*) This is Maria, my friend of about ten years. Maria and I met doing a community theatre production of *Annie* where we both played unnamed orphans. This may seem like a detail that compromises her anonymity, but I've played an unnamed orphan in multiple community theatre productions of *Annie*. We're both twenty-two, having dinner at my apartment.

ELLIE
(*to MARIA*) I don't know if I told you this – when this Jian thing broke, I was in this kind-of-relationship with this guy in my class. He was like, um, he had a shirt that said "This Is What a Feminist Looks Like" and all his close friends were girls, and he was raised by a single mom and just a super-chill guy, way more PC than I am. And, um, and then we would have sex, and he was super violent, and then it would finish, and it was almost to the moment that it would finish, he would change. So, like, he would do aggressive things during sex and also just little gross oversteps, things you should probably ask before doing. Like, he'd cum in my face, without any warning, you know.

MARIA
Ugh.

ELLIE
Right?! And like, right away, he'd get up and get a paper towel and give it to me, and he'd tend to it immediately and

I'd clean myself up, you know, there was no lingering in the moment. He'd do it and –

MARIA
It was done.

ELLIE
Yeah, it was as if he felt embarrassed by what had happened.

MARIA
Yeah.

ELLIE
Yeah, "Jack," giving him the name "Jack," yeah, um, one night, in second year, I remember, he came over, and we were drunk – and, um, he'd also come over sometimes and we'd just cuddle. We had that, and the line between friendship and relationship was seriously blurred because we also just hung out in a platonic way pretty often. So he came over and I didn't want to have sex because I noticed this pattern where our friendship took a week or so to recover after we would sleep together, and I didn't want to take the chance of alienating him, and he seemed to become distant after we'd have sex. So, he was trying to – you know, he was really drunk, I was really drunk, he was trying to go down on me, just trying to get me into it, and I was like, "No, I really don't want to – I just feel like you get awkward with me after we have sex," and he was like, "Well, is this any less awkward?" And I thought, "Well, maybe not." And then by the end of it, we ended up having sex, and that was like, the most aggressive sex that we'd ever had, and he, like, he put his forearm over my neck and leaned down quite hard –

MARIA
And choked you?

ELLIE
Yeah, but it was kind of like – "Okay, even if I wanted to say 'Stop,' I can't, because you're choking me, and I can't actually take a breath in, like, in order to speak." And then he kept putting his hand over my face and, like, crushing my face. And I was like, well this is a bit weird, you know, it just went a bit far. Oh, God.

MARIA
No, no, it's okay.

ELLIE
Yeah. Confusing with the feminist stuff, though.

MARIA
Yeah. 'Cause you're a feminist?

ELLIE
No, I mean, 'cause he so is, and Jian, just didn't expect – and I remember trying to be like, "So is that what – like, what are you into?" And he just didn't wanna talk about sex when we –

MARIA
Weren't having sex.

ELLIE
Yeah. But when we were having sex... Oh, man. Lots of "fucks," lots of "whore," lots of "fucking whore," and then he'd say, like, "Say something to me" and I'd be like... "Ahh! Boo! Fuck you!"

MARIA
You should have been like, "Fuck you, you fucking moron!" Really throw him off.

ELLIE
Ha ha ha. Yeah.

MARIA
The word "fuck" is such a weird word. It's just such a gross word. I use it because I'm not sure what else to. And sometimes it's fine and in some contexts it's wrong, but then what do you say? "Make love" is too weird. You don't want to say that.

ELLIE
Nope. So, as one of my only friends my age in a very long-term relationship, what do you say?

MARIA
I think "have sex" is pretty adequate. Although if I wanna have sex, I usually say to Tyler, "Do you wanna snuggle?" and it's just become code for me asking for sex: I ask and he knows I'm down. Although then it means we basically can never just snuggle. We have no term for that.

SCENE 4

ELLIE

(*to the audience*) This is me on Skype with my fifty-something friend, Jimmy.

JIMMY

(*to ELLIE*) Hey, girl – good to see you! Gorgeous as ever.

ELLIE

(*to JIMMY*) Hi! Same to you! How's it going?

JIMMY

So we're doing this with our shirts on? Just kidding.

ELLIE

Ha – how are you?

JIMMY

I'm good. So, this is documentary theatre?

ELLIE

Yeah, so I'm recording this, is that okay?

JIMMY

Yeah. And it's about sex? Kinky sex.

ELLIE

Well, the Jian story is the starting point, but I want it to be more generally about the ways in which we communicate consent.

JIMMY

So, why me? Ha ha.

ELLIE
Well, let's see, Jimmy, you're a former-reverend-turned-pimp-turned-devoted-dad. I thought you might have a unique perspective.

JIMMY
Not quite right, I just worked for a pimp. I was... I was thinking about this stuff a bit when you sent me that message. I was thinking about the stripper from Wisconsin that I dated, remember her?

ELLIE
A bit.

JIMMY
Yeah. Well. We were involved back in the day, fifteen years ago? Before I met my wife and then – I don't wanna give her name, let's call her Christie, the stripper, she had this ex... Many exes, I guess, that were... abusive and dangerous even after the relationships were over. I was in the firing line a bit as the new guy, and so Christie and I were very off-and-on-again. Well, Christie – I started to realize with her and with all the women I met... The women who I met who worked in the sex trade were almost always involved with scary men... I'm scared to say this, because it sounds dangerously like victim blaming, but these are women who have been sexually abused again and again at different points in their lives and by different people. I remember one chick, she just opened up to me when she was wasted and told me about being raped as a little kid in an ongoing way by her brother and then going to live with her grandparents and getting into the church community there and being raped again by someone else there, then in her early twenties by another guy in another town, just the same episode repeating itself. And when we spoke, she – I just remember thinking, "What terrible luck."

ELLIE
   Yeah!

JIMMY
   Well, yeah. But, then I lived a bit more, and it's not as simple as terrible luck. It's like, these women, who are repeatedly abused, like they have the scent of prey, and these men, the predators, can sniff out prey. And to me, I'm not a predator, so I can't tell these women immediately because I'm not attuned to that, but over time I saw that. And I think the men that hurt these women were almost certainly abused in childhood, too. Obviously, there are exceptions to this, but I think women abused as kids grow up to marry men who hit them and men abused as kids are those men. I read something on Facebook about how the brains of abused children resemble the brains of soldiers who've gotten back from combat.

ELLIE
   PTSD.

JIMMY
   But a very specific kind of PTSD, where they can anticipate pain, they're wired for that – a survival instinct, but when there's no need, it makes them anxious and depressed, right? And so, with that they want someone they perceive as strong and certain – but certainty doesn't really exist. And those who seem absolutely certain are usually the most lost of them all. So, these women are attracted to these douchebags who are really just... controlling, not certain, just controlling.

ELLIE
   So, this scent that these women have, the scent of prey...

JIMMY
   I can't say much more about it. Because I can't smell it.

SCENE 5

RADIO HOST sits inside a sound booth, live on air, speaking with a WOMAN by phone.

RADIO HOST
We have now reached a woman who claims she was attacked by Jian Ghomeshi. She's not one of the four women that have gone to the *Star*. We've agreed not to use her real name.

WOMAN
I met Jian about – it was over ten years ago, and it was at a Christmas media party. And at the party, he was smitten by me, and I was taken with his charm. I was just coming out of a relationship, a very long one, so I hadn't dated in a while, and I was liking the attention – and just thought he was a very charming man.

He first asked me to come to a taping of his show. And I did. And... there was nothing to give me any indication that there was anything wrong. We stayed around and chatted with some of his colleagues after the taping, then we went off alone and were chatting in his car. Then he asked me if I would undo my buttons, and I said "no" and he reached over and grabbed my hair very hard and pulled my head back. And it really threw me off. And I don't know, really, exactly what he was saying, but I'm thinking it was something along the lines of, "Do you like this?" and I... I don't know what I said. But it was a weeknight, and it was late, and I had to go. I'd never experienced anything like this. I didn't like it – that's not my style. And also – I was thinking, "Did I miss something, not dating for a while?" I kinda put it to – that, if a couple gets together there's always a little learning curve and it could be – don't hit me too hard, or, don't kiss me like that. I was more shy, and I just thought, "I'll figure it out later." I hadn't dated in a while, and I did like him, and all the time I spent with him up to that point was great. There was nothing about him that I didn't like. And that – I thought, maybe he's just a little too rough, and I can sort it out. I come from an educated family, I thought, "Wow, that's a guy my dad would really like!"

SCENE 6

ELLIE and HOPE sit at a kitchen table.

HOPE
Ellie, just stop. It's charging. I told you. Can you please just stop?

ELLIE
(*to the audience*) I have sisters, but I'd never ever talked to them about sex. Until this project. This is me with my sixteen-year-old sister, Hope, in the house we grew up in, in / Kingsville, Ontario.

HOPE
It's fine, Ellie, it's fine. You're so annoying… (*sighing*)

ELLIE
(*to HOPE*) So, what was your reaction to the Jian story breaking?

HOPE
Well, I don't know. I mean, I know he was just, like, pretending as if, like, he, um, like, he just has weird fetishes, like, I remember that a lot, and I was just like, "Okay, that's bullshit." Like… like, when was *Fifty Shades of Grey* released, was it around the same time?

ELLIE
He references *Fifty Shades* in his Facebook post.

HOPE
Does he?

ELLIE
Yeah.

HOPE
I mean, *Fifty Shades of Grey*, on the topic of BDSM, as well, but also not proper BDSM, because the way the BDSM community works is, like –

RICHARD pops in.

RICHARD
Have you talked to her about this?

ELLIE
What, Dad? No, I have not talked to Hopey about BDSM.

RICHARD
Well, she has very interesting things to say about it.

ELLIE
What is happening?

RICHARD
I'm going now! Carry on!

RICHARD exits.

HOPE
Well, I did a lot of research when *Fifty Shades* came out, like the book, and like, I read a bunch of posts from people who actually, like, did BDSM, because they were very offended that their – community? I don't know if you would say – was being represented this way. Because what they say is that their trusting of the other partner is very, very deep, because you have to have that, like, much of a connection with that person to (*laughing*) to allow them to do those kinds of things. And, uh, there's always, like, a safe word that

you have to rely on, that's, like, one of the most important things, 'cause it can get way too far for one person, and that's not then consensual, like, completely, (*laughing a bit*) which then means it's rape, right? But, like, and so, like, there's obviously, like, people on the outside are like, Oh BDSM, that's crazy, that's a really weird thing to be into, and if you don't know anything, you think, like, all BDSM is choking and like, whipping and whatever, but like, there's a lot more to it than that.

ELLIE
Like what?

HOPE
Like what I just said.

ELLIE
Oh okay, sorry. (*pause*) This is obviously totally weird to talk to you about, but all sorts of people don't identify with the BDSM community but would have elements of that kind of stuff in their sex life. Ideas of dominance and submission are no longer niche, if they ever were, you know, so, um, so, what about sex that's not within the BDSM community, someone just consents to, like –

HOPE
Like, just?

ELLIE
So, I'm – I'm not asking if this has come up for you yet, I don't know if I wanna know, but hypothetically, and, you know, you have older friends, hypothetically, how would you give someone your consent?

HOPE
Well, I hope they would ask. (*smiling and laughing awkwardly*) And I would say yes.

ELLIE
So they would say, like, "Can we have sex?" and you would say "Yes"?

HOPE
Well, not even, I mean, that sounds, like, so awkward.

ELLIE
I know!

HOPE
But like, I mean, 'cause like – but it's not even, 'cause like, initially, yeah – as a teenager, you wanna have that conversation with the person you wanna do it with for the first time. You're gonna be like, "So do you wanna start doing it?" right? And that's, like, obviously the first step of consent, but just saying that you will consent for a further occurrence of sex isn't actually – like, for consent to be actually, like, good, it needs to be ongoing.

ELLIE
So how do you communicate when it's changed? (*pause*) I mean, I'll say, I've had situations where I've wanted to stop, and I have not felt comfortable saying "Can we stop?" And these are with really nice people, who would have stopped without any problem. But I felt that the discomfort of continuing would be less than the discomfort of asking to stop. You know?

HOPE
I mean, I do know somebody who, their first time was probably kinda rape, because I mean, she kept doing it afterward, 'cause then she was consensual afterward. But for the first time I know she was – I mean, this is a friend of a friend, so it's third-hand information – but I know she did say that her friend, she didn't even know if she wanted to have sex yet for the first time then. But she was very, like,

ambiguous about it, 'cause she didn't really know what had happened, but like, it was her and her boyfriend, and she didn't really want to do it –

ELLIE
Was alcohol involved?

HOPE
Yeah, yeah, but like, she continued doing it afterward, and (*laughing*) she really enjoyed it afterward. But the initial thing was – probably – (*laughing*) rapey. So, like, yeah – it's just complicated. So I feel like, I would hope that I would be with somebody who I would feel comfortable enough with to say, like, "No." But yeah, you would consent to the initial act, then you would hope you could say no, for the consent to be – continual.

ELLIE
Yeah. Definitely. Okay. Okay.

SCENE 7

ELLIE

(*to the audience*) What I said about my sisters, about not talking to them about sex, is actually true for me with my female friends generally. We never really spoke of sex in any detail until I initiated these conversations for the play. This is my very good friend of a very long time, Sophie. She's twenty-three.

SOPHIE

(*to ELLIE*) Aggressive?

ELLIE

(*to SOPHIE*) Yeah.

SOPHIE

I'm completely cool with that. I actually like aggression. But a lot of guys, it's really strange, even if I give my permission, and even if I'm, like, stone-cold sober and I'm like, "Listen, I am giving you permission to be aggressive," I feel like a lot of the time they're just like, "No, no, but, uh, I'm going to hurt you." And I'm like, "No, listen: it's okay." And then even afterward, after they've done it, it's like they feel they've abused you in some way, even if you agreed to it. And it's like, I'm not going to change my mind! If I was uncomfortable, like, while this was going on, I would have said something like "Stop," you know?

ELLIE

Yeah.

SOPHIE
And it's kind of scary, because it's like, how much is too much? Well, I would tell you. But I guess they're worried that you're not going to tell them and that you would go too far. But it's actually funny, because in some cases, like, I've – like – I've, freaked the shit out of some people – because, like, I like, I'll be like, "No, go for it, like, really go for it." And I would wake up with bruises or I'll, like – I'll, like, be … bleeding or something. And they'll be like "What, wha, wha?" And I'll be like, "No, okay, fine, look at me, do I look upset? No! Okay, far from upset!" I'm not gonna leave and change my mind!

ELLIE
Yeah.

SOPHIE
You know what the funny thing is? I think that aggression and sex are two very natural things and they sort of come hand in hand in some ways. And if people can acknowledge that these impulses exist, they can – you know, people are ashamed of wanting these things, they beat themselves up – ha ha, sorry, strange choice of expression there.

ELLIE laughs.

SOPHIE
The choking thing, I like, the choking thing I have had done to me – or wanted it done to me. Not so much so that I pass out.

ELLIE
How do you ask for it? Is it awkward? Do you bring it up before hand or during?

SOPHIE

Um... No, not before. During. I just – from the way I've done it so far, I just literally take his hands, and I put them on my neck, and I make him squeeze. And he's just like, "What?" And I don't even say anything. 'Cause if you're going to ease someone into it... And I remember one time, you know, he was like, "You want me to choke you?" And I was like, "Yes!" And he never held too long and... I feel a bit guilty, I guess. Because I think I pressured him into doing things to me that he would have otherwise not felt comfortable doing. And I put him in the position of dominance. I put him there, and I think he might have felt obliged to maintain it. And the problem is, I asked for all of this, but I would never want to do that to somebody. So it's unfair. And a lot of the time – he tried to get me to do stuff in public places, but because of my own sense of, I don't know, propriety, I didn't do it. But I really wanted to do it. And I think he knew that, because he kept trying and then... I started being brave enough to give into it. And, well, for me, that was good. But it's confusing. I'm hearing myself and I'm basically saying that coercion was a good thing for me. But I know – it's not for everyone. Just hard to navigate. Okay, okay, this is fun, ask me something else!

SCENE 8

ELLIE
(*to the audience*) I have a lot of close male friends, but I was having a hard time getting them to be open with me. I thought if I found some guys I wasn't friends with to talk with, I might get somewhere. I found these two on a film set for a film about frat guys and sorority girls. I played a sorority girl. They played frat guys. They're actors. We were sitting around a table, all dressed the part.

WILLIAM
(*to ELLIE*) You'll need to understand, Ellie.

ELLIE
(*to WILLIAM*) Yeah.

WILLIAM
That when a man has an orgasm it's really incredible and it feels exceptional, until the second it's over, and then he instantaneously feels paramount amounts of guilt and shame –

ELLIE
What? Do you agree with this?

BEN
More or less.

WILLIAM
And thinks to himself, "What have I done? What would my mother say?"

ELLIE
Ugh.

WILLIAM
And then, he rolls over and makes a sandwich –

BEN
It's just that after that release, all sexual desire is gone for a few seconds.

ELLIE
And shame is there to replace it?

WILLIAM
Yeah.

ELLIE
Jesus.

BEN
It's just that once you ejaculate, yeah, all desire is gone for a few moments, and so if your only interest in the person is sexual – it's weird. But it comes back, the desire.

WILLIAM
Yeah, yeah. Exactly. Like, am I just using this person's body?

ELLIE
Okay, okay.

WILLIAM
And here's another thing. With guys, they're never reticent when it comes to having sex. With women, there's always an element of "No means maybe."

BEN
Because female biology is such that – I mean, right? – it takes longer for women to get warmed up, so, coercion can be, successful, right? Is this really offensive?

ELLIE
Nah. I remember with my serious ex, he had more of a drive than me, and I remember me not feeling up for it and him persuading me, just, you know, turning me on with little acts of foreplay, and then I was up for it, and when we were finished, I said something totally – ha ha, I can't put this in the play – something like, "Never let me say no again," or something.

WILLIAM
Feminist Ellie Moon, everyone!

ELLIE
Terrible.

WILLIAM
No, but exactly.

SCENE 9

ELLIE
(*to the audience*) This is Dana. She's the hairstylist on that film. She's in her late thirties. (*to DANA*) Most of the women I speak to, they describe an experience where it's not that they said no, and their partner continued, and it's not even that they were in a situation where they felt they couldn't say no, it's like – they were in a situation where it didn't feel worth it to say no.

DANA
(*to ELLIE*) Hmm. Yeah. I know that feeling.

DANA
You should unpick that idea of "worth it." A lot there in the idea of whether it's worth the consequence of saying no, the risk of being seen as a schoolmarm.

    Beat.

ELLIE
The amount that guys check in with me during sex since I've started this project is a bit nuts. The guys I've been with in that time, I'll tell them I'm working on this project... I don't go out of my way to, it just comes up –

DANA
Woah, no pun intended – sorry. Yeah, they check in, that's sweet though.

ELLIE
Oh, it is.

DANA
You date nice guys.

ELLIE
I do.

DANA
But when men are checking in all the time ensuring the consent is ongoing, right, it takes you out of the moment?

ELLIE
Maybe, I don't know.

DANA
Too bad intuiting is a female thing.

ELLIE
Really? Do you think that?

DANA
Yeah. Lesbians don't have consent issues.

ELLIE
I will fact-check that.

DANA
I've been, certainly, having sex before and not been into it and he doesn't notice. Right, and that probably isn't the case for my male partners. It's just a lack of intuition, I think, and, like – and, a lack of intuition isn't rape.

ELLIE
No. But I'm not looking for what is rape and what isn't. More like, what creates this distance –

DANA
I think everything is just ambiguous and mysterious and sex is just part of that and consent is all just part of that. But maybe the ambiguity is part of what's good about sex, 'cause, you know, if you take the ambiguity out of art, it sucks – so, like, maybe it's the same with sex.

ELLIE
So maybe I'm ruining sex for myself?

DANA
Nah, I'm talking shit – you can't take the ambiguity out of anything. It's there, no matter. I do think, though, you get older, you get less weird about communicating, you get more confident and communication and confidence, that helps sex a lot, and that's also what's lacking in young people, right? So we can all expect our sex to get better as we get older. Just less frequent. Kidding. Maybe.

> *DANA pulls out a bottle of hairspray and sprays for a while.*

DANA
Okay. You're done.

ELLIE
(*reaching up to pat her hair*) Thanks. And, thanks.

DANA
My pleasure. Don't touch your hair.

ELLIE
Sorry.

SCENE 10

ELLIE
(*to the audience*) Mitch responded to my Facebook request for interviews, and we had a really long conversation where he talked about toxic monogamy culture. We had just finished an interview in his apartment – which is just a bed and a sink – sitting on the end of his bed.

ELLIE
(*to MITCH*) Thanks for talking to me about that. Getting everyone's stories, such a cool privilege.

MITCH starts kissing ELLIE's arm.

MITCH
(*to ELLIE*) What do people say?

ELLIE
What y'doing?

MITCH
I'm giving you my consent.

ELLIE
Oh, right. Ha ha. (*now uncomfortable with the kissing, shutting it down*) Hey – hey – tickles.

MITCH
How come that never happens, huh, no one ever worries about whether a dude's consented, why do you think that is?

ELLIE
(*closing herself off*) I don't know, maybe – I've actually been thinking about that.

MITCH
Come here.

ELLIE
(*moving away from him*) I was thinking about that question –

MITCH
– It's just because of the biology – the man penetrates the woman, so the implication of power... You know what I mean? So... may I penetrate you?

ELLIE
No.

MITCH
Is it because I said "penetrate"?

ELLIE
No.

MITCH
Was that at least part of it?

ELLIE
(*not entirely convincingly*) ... No. We're friends, Mitch.

MITCH
But we both just acknowledged our ability to extend friendships and to still remain... friends.

ELLIE

I just don't – see it that way with you. I think we shouldn't. For now, at least. I'm sorry.

MITCH

It's fine. Of course it's fine. Thought this play idea might be indicative of some sexual frustration, that's all. Is it hard for women to initiate sex, have you found that, as a lady person?

Beat.

ELLIE

Um, I don't know. I guess so. It's awkward. I don't know if it's harder than it is for guys, though. It's just generally hard, isn't it?

ELLIE and MITCH sit in silence for a moment.

SCENE 11

ELLIE

(*to the audience*) Josie was the first person to like the Facebook post I put out requesting interview subjects. She was the shy kid in our class growing up, so we all kind of used her as a prop in our conversations, but there was one day in grade four where it was a busses-cancelled kind of snow day, so a class of, like, six people, and we got to just play games in the gym all day, and Josie went wild. Maniacally laughing, and instructing us all in a game involving scooter boards and lacrosse nets. And then the next day she was back in her shell. And stayed there for me, basically, until this interview.

JOSIE

(*to ELLIE*) Y'know Ellie, I know you're not going to like this. I feel like such a bad feminist saying this...

ELLIE

(*to JOSIE*) Go ahead, I'm changing everyone's names anyway.

JOSIE

Yeah, so, I would never say this non-anonymously but, like, I haven't been raped and I totally consider that a huge privilege and, or whatever, but I've been very lucky, certainly. But I also believe, I just, I don't believe that that is only luck, that there is no connection between my never being raped and my never getting drunk at parties and sleeping in beds with strangers. I don't wanna be fucking smug, but I never did that shit, and I never got raped at a party. Or even close. I had those experiences as a young, young kid – like, five, six – and um, it did then, as it does, it did for me, um, set off a sort of pattern. I definitely did, um, then have a long period of time in which I was reenacting trauma, like, going back in so I could figure it out and get it right, with different people, but back into similar situations, I mean. Seeking out controlling and manipulative partners. And there was a kind of reprogramming I had to do, um, building new habits, what that requires, we've all done it, we've all had to. And that's not to victim blame at all. I think, well, I blame my parents. (*laughing*)

Yeah, but I don't know how helpful that is to your play. When I was a kid, the stuff that happened, it's obviously quite clear-cut because I was a kid. But, I was, like, very interested in what was happening at the time, and the abuse, it gave me a sense of importance and it was exciting. It was attention, I was a kid. But of course, just because I experienced it, positively, like I was into it in many ways, um, back then, doesn't meant it was for the right reasons and wasn't ultimately deeply damaging and totally an assault. But similarly, just because someone has a negative experience, doesn't make it, um, do you – you know?

ELLIE
Maybe? Can you say more about that?

JOSIE
I don't know, I feel a sort of resistance to where the conversation has gone, hmm – maybe I'm smug because my abuse was worse, because I was a kid? I know that's not helpful, but I'm just, if I'm being honest. And honesty is helpful, maybe. Ha. I mean, you know me, right, I go out and I drink, but with people I know. To get blackout drunk with, like, a hundred or more basically totally anonymous people? I am skeptical of whatever's at the root of that desire, honestly. I know this sounds like victim blaming. Yikes. But, like, have you even gotten drunk and slept in a stranger's bed?

ELLIE
I – I don't, hmmm – I mean, not really a stranger.

JOSIE
A dude should obviously never take advantage of a drunk girl, but I know how I am when I get wasted, I wanna fuck everything, right?

ELLIE
Yeah? I'm not really like that when I drink.

JOSIE
No? Just, when I was doing long-distance with Freddie, I didn't get wasted at parties, ever, really, 'cause I knew if I did, my chances of cheating on him would be great. Or, if I would go out and drink, it would only be at parties with people who I knew I wasn't attracted to.

ELLIE
How do you find those parties?

JOSIE
Gatherings. Small get-togethers.

ELLIE
Right.

JOSIE
I just... think it all got messed up – women should have the right to say no to sex, be that with a stranger or their husband, whatever, but to get blackout drunk at a party, sleep with someone, have it be awful either at the time or after the fact, have a complicated, shameful relationship with it, regret it, and then absolve ourselves of the whole thing because we were drunk, so it was rape? 'Cause we didn't consent? Seems – don't know.

ELLIE
But – does anyone feel absolved, you said "absolved," right? Yeah, or even just remotely better off at all, by deciding they were victimized? I don't think so –

JOSIE
Why not? It means it was out of your control, as opposed to that you failed in some responsibility to yourself.

ELLIE
I think most people would wanna feel they were in control, though, and even take a failing on the chin for that control, that's why people are often in denial about this stuff for so long. But, no, sorry, how does your experience, um, inform –

JOSIE
Yeah, I felt shame, with my abuse. I was interested in what was happening, excited by the attention, then I was told by him, um, that if I ever told anyone, you know, not to because it's bad, and – that's when I felt the shame. At that point. And I saw it as something bad I was involved in, not something done to me. And discovering as an adult that actually I was a kid – has let me, let go of the shame. But, in exchange, it's traumatic to decide you had no control, yeah, my parents didn't protect me, and I wasn't safe to all sorts of things, as well as that, then. I guess you're right. And it made me want to – yes, like I say, like, get with someone controlling, but be able to maintain some control in those relationships, I've had to get over that. Look at what I do and ask why and stop and I just don't know... where protecting women ends and infantilizing them begins. My situation is unique. Probably everyone says that.

ELLIE
So, is it the institutional, legal kind of structures that are in place right now that you feel are infantilizing, or the language of the conversation itself, or –

JOSIE

    I just don't know if it is right that so many women walk around feeling victimized from these drunken sexual encounters deemed "rapes," when the communication was probably poor and ambiguous and unsatisfying for both parties? I care about women, I don't blame them for the societal conditioning that makes them think they have to self-objectify or drink to keep up at parties or whatever, but this is a new kind of conditioning of women we're seeing now in the #ibelievewomen world. It's conditioning victimization. I know trauma, and trauma is real. Yeah, sexual guilt and shame is, that's, like, real and women can absolve themselves of responsibility – but in exchange for choosing trauma, the trauma of deciding you were powerless. And deciding you're powerless can perpetuate powerlessness. It did for me. The rush to diagnose trauma, and yes, are we just giving women trauma starter packs through, through paternalistic systems, that's not an empowering, like, landscape, or whatever, in my opinion. Yeah, drunk girls at college. They can absolve themselves of responsibility or shame – which lots of people of both genders really strive to do – by classifying the experience as out of their control, as I said, right? And control without responsibility: every adult of any gender's dream.

SCENE 12

ELLIE
(to the audience) This is Martha Shaffer. She's a professor of criminal law at the University of Toronto. We spoke in her office.

MARTHA SHAFFER
(to ELLIE) The thing about consent as it relates to criminal law is that, in criminal law, to find someone guilty of an offence, you need to find two things – you need to find that someone has committed the physical act, or the *actus reus*, and that they have the necessary mental element – we call that the *mens rea*. So, if there was touching without consent, obviously right there we have the *actus reus* – the physical act of the offence. But even where it's clear the complainant did not consent, if the accused doesn't have the *mens rea*, the mental element to sexually assault, the accused is not guilty. The accused must be aware of non-consent, for there to be *mens rea* for there to be guilt. I'm trying to make this – 'cause you can't put this in a play, no one's gonna understand this –

ELLIE
(to MARTHA SHAFFER) No, no, that's okay, people kinda like to be confused by plays –

MARTHA SHAFFER
Yeah? So, the way the Supreme Court has interpreted consent is to say, whether or not the complainant agrees on being touched is purely in the mind of the complainant – it's what's in her mind, she doesn't have to show her non-consent, she doesn't have to vocalize her non-consent, if she didn't consent in her mind, there is no consent. Which is good, but can be a problem. So, you don't consent, but you don't say you're

not consenting, you don't show it. That other person who is touching you may quite legitimately think, because we do gauge consent based on the behaviour, that person may actually think you're consenting. We don't wanna say, "You can't make a mistake about consent," right, I think we wanna say, "You can't make an unreasonable mistake about consent," which is why honest but mistaken belief is a defence, but we had a reform, so now a requirement to show that one took reasonable steps to assess consent, if one wants to use that defence. But to be honest, most of the time, where consent isn't being given – unless you are in fear for your safety, unless you freeze, which sometimes people do –

ELLIE
Yeah! –

MARTHA SHAFFER
But most of the time, you will communicate your non-consent if you are not consenting.

ELLIE
Oh, yeah? I don't know.

MARTHA SHAFFER
Most of the time.

ELLIE
Yeah, I mean, you'd know of more cases than I would.

MARTHA SHAFFER
So that's the law as it's supposed to be applied, but, of course, law is always applied within the backdrop of myth and stereotype, you always have the backdrop of sexism, the judges and juries who are reading this within that context. I do think the law itself is good, it's gonna be mostly about education of judges and defence counsel. And sex ed. But also just... time. Like, lots of time. Many more generations.

SCENE 13

As in the opening scene, the actors take their places and share delivery of the interviewee's words. They use their own voices to do so, not altering their own speech.

RADIO VOICE
Another woman has come forward to the CBC to talk about her encounters with Jian Ghomeshi. The woman is in her twenties and lives in southeastern New Brunswick. She contacted us to tell her story, and I recorded an interview with her yesterday. A warning to sensitive listeners – parts of her story are graphic and disturbing. She asked that we protect her identity, and we have altered her voice for this interview.

NEW BRUNSWICK WOMAN (ELLIE)
I met him at the book signing he had here in 2012. After he had his little talk, he decided to sign everyone's books. And I was in line, and he signed my book. When he was signing my book – he started asking a lot of personal questions about me, my name – what's my name, what's my last name, what do I do for a living, and I noticed he wrote it down on a little Post-it. And I was being fairly flirty in return, and I said, "I have Facebook, by the way," and then we left it at that. And that evening he contacted me on Facebook with his phone number and told me to text him.

RADIO VOICE
What did you think?

NEW BRUNSWICK WOMAN (SECOND ACTOR)
I was excited. I thought, why me – of all the people in the book signing? I felt very excited. I went to dinner with him. We went back to his hotel room – nothing sexual happened in his hotel room. He came off a little aggressive, not overly aggressive, and I remember he said, "I can be aggressive, don't let it scare you," and I took his word on it. And we parted ways and continued to talk over text and telephone. And then I went to see him in Toronto a couple weeks later.

RADIO VOICE
So, what happened in Toronto?

NEW BRUNSWICK WOMAN (THIRD ACTOR)
Um, I took a cab to his house from the airport. I knocked on his door. He opened the door and I was smiling, happy to see him, saying hello. Expected to maybe have a tour of his house, have a hello from him, "Would you like something to eat? How was your flight?" Normal conversation. Um, but, he pushed me against the wall, immediately, um, started making out with me. And then he led me upstairs and told me to get on my knees and then, uh, proceeded to hit me very hard across the head, a few times, to the point where I couldn't see straight, my vision was blurred.

RADIO VOICE
What was going through your mind then?

NEW BRUNSWICK WOMAN (FOURTH ACTOR)
Shock. I had no idea, um, he spoke over text about – he had these violent types of tendencies. And when I started to back off when he said these things over text, he called me to assure me that none of this would happen in real life, if I was uncomfortable to tell him, but this was pure text fantasy. And so, when he was violent with me without any talk of it ahead of time, at his house, I didn't see it coming, it blindsided me. After that, he took his belt off,

put it around my neck, and started leading me around his hallway and bedroom, and he was pulling really hard at my neck. Then he took it off and started beating me in the back with it.

RADIO VOICE
What were you saying to him at the time?

NEW BRUNSWICK WOMAN (ELLIE)
Nothing. I was in so much shock – and I've heard this from other women who are speaking as well – I did not know what to say. It totally threw me for a loop. I was speechless.

RADIO VOICE
So how long did this continue?

NEW BRUNSWICK WOMAN (SECOND ACTOR)
I would say the whole violence aspect of it lasted about twenty, thirty minutes.

RADIO VOICE
And how did it end?

NEW BRUNSWICK WOMAN (THIRD ACTOR)
We ended up having intercourse. And then it just came to an end that way.

RADIO VOICE
So you left the house?

NEW BRUNSWICK WOMAN (FOURTH ACTOR)
Um, I stayed at his house. I was staying at his house, he had invited me to stay at his house. I didn't have anywhere to go.

RADIO VOICE
That's why you stayed, you had nowhere else to go?

NEW BRUNSWICK WOMAN (ELLIE)
I didn't know Toronto. Um, I had nowhere else to go. (*pause*) And as soon as he was done that, he was nice and friendly and normal, again. It's as if something switches when the violence starts, and he changes, and then after that he's a normal guy, doing normal activities, after that.

SCENE 14

TYLER
(*to ELLIE*) Is this for your play – ?

ELLIE
(*to the audience*) This is Tyler. He's a police officer, he's the boyfriend of a good friend. He's twenty-seven. I was actually staying at their place at the time, so this was in their kitchen.

ELLIE
(*to TYLER*) Yeah, for the play.

TYLER
Right. Can you record me?

ELLIE
I'm already recording.

TYLER
I'll talk. We like to paint rapists as "monsters" because it makes us feel comfortable, because lovely humans like us would never do such things, right, and if you start to think of men who rape as victims who could have been helped, well, then we worry that we're excusing them for their actions, but we're not. It's not good enough to, like, "teach men not to rape," people don't just rape because they don't understand consent. If we can help men who are victims of sexual abuse before they themselves perpetuate the cycle of abuse, we might do a better job of stopping it. But to do that, we have to start acknowledging the humanity of abusers. No one is born one, they are created, sadly, right? And the fact that your play will basically only cover the experiences of women and not delve into how common it is for men to

be sexually assaulted and never come forward, well, you're perpetuating the very thing you're trying to combat. Your play isn't balanced. It's about what bad things men do to women – where is the equality in that? Inequality caused this. And equality could fix it, I think.

ELLIE
I agree.

TYLER
We just have different terms for it, that's all.

ELLIE
In what way?

TYLER
Feminism.

ELLIE
Feminism, yes, is a term that means equality.

TYLER
Equality means equality. Feminists don't want equality, they want preference. It's in the title, "fem-." It's like, radical feminists who believe in tipping the scale until it's balanced, right? I do think they're the main perpetuators of rape culture. They aim to completely emasculate men, shut down any real discussion, all while denying any of the abuse men have suffered or any of men's vulnerabilities. And they wonder why men become hostile and serially rape women? Sorry, but like, at least women's voices are being heard when they suffer sexual abuse now, but until we hear the voices of men who've suffered in the same way, we won't be fixing it. You can't ignore half the problem. I also think that had Jian been gay, the same things would have happened to men. And we don't know it didn't happen to more men, even. His story is pure power. Not about gender.

ELLIE
Okay. You don't think there are aspects in which gender and power are still tied? Do you wanna say more about that?

TYLER
No. And, actually – one thing, wait, wait! – personally, as someone who argues with feminists – I don't identify as a men's rights activist but I am also not a feminist, I'm an arguer with feminism, and well – it's nice to see a staunch male feminist get caught abusing women.

ELLIE
Is it? Is it nice, Tyler?

TYLER
Shut up, I'm saying that men who are opposed to aspects or the whole of the construction of feminism are, are the guys who everyone thinks hit women. And Jian was above suspicion, as a self-proclaimed feminist, right? Wasn't he? Isn't that a big part of why this is so shocking? And it's sort of, yes, nice, for someone like me, who has to worry that these views I have – these non-simplistic, antifundamentalist, maybe, views I have, I have to worry that people will listen only to a slice of what my position is and assume I fall into the bad side of the, you know, apparently two sides. The pressure these dudes feel toward sensitivity, not true sensitivity, where you judge moment-to-moment, but "sensitivity," like, saying, "I'm an ally." This compounds resentments men have toward women, they already don't feel taken care of, because they aren't, and they need to pretend to have these views they never question, to even be acceptable. Shaming men and protecting women isn't working.

ELLIE
So, men feel ashamed to be men? That exists?

TYLER
Yeah, because "rape culture" is on us. Right?

ELLIE
No –

TYLER
Yeah, we talk about this only in a gendered way. We just spend straight up too much time considering gender, and feminism only contributes to that. The feminist "dialogue" has a clear place they are placing blame, and it causes dudes to feel ashamed.

SCENE 15

ELLIE is naked and in bed with YAO.
They're building up to something.

ELLIE
(*to the audience*) I met Yao at a birthday party for a mutual friend, and this was captured later on the evening.

YAO
(*to ELLIE*) So, what do you like, Ellie Moon?

ELLIE
I – I don't know. I'm still figuring it out.

YAO
What have you figured out so far?

ELLIE
I don't know. I'm okay with what's going on presently.

YAO
All right.

ELLIE
What do you like?

YAO
I like you. You're sexy.

ELLIE
You're sexy, too.

YAO
Oh, you flatter. What's your number?

ELLIE
You have my number.

YAO
Number of sexual partners.

ELLIE
Oh. That's hard. It's hard to remember – give me a sec. Seven? Give or take. Hard to remember when you actually did the deed, isn't it?

YAO
The deed?

ELLIE
Sex.

YAO
You call it that?

ELLIE
What do you call it?

YAO
Sex. Have you ever orgasmed?

ELLIE
Of course.

YAO
Do you touch yourself?

ELLIE
Of course.

YAO
How often?

ELLIE
I don't know.

YAO
What do you do? Can you show me? I'm making you shy, aren't I?

ELLIE
Yup. But remember what you said earlier? You don't believe in shyness.

YAO
I don't not believe in it. I just think it's an excuse.

ELLIE
You never have a situation where you feel paralyzed? You just can't will yourself to go up to someone or assert something, like your body stops you, even though your mind might really want to?

YAO
Of course, but I don't think that's shyness. That's something else that that person needs to figure out. That's being a grown-up, doing uncomfortable things sometimes. (*referring to a touch*) Do you like that?

ELLIE
Yeah. What's your number?

YAO
Um. One sec. Twenty-one.

ELLIE
Good number.

YAO
Yeah. Do you like that?

ELLIE
Yeah.

YAO
Sex is different for women. Took me a while to get that. Pain and pleasure are more closely linked for women, it's not like that for men. Do you cum easily?

ELLIE
Oh, um. I'm not sure what to compare it to. I think so, yeah. Why?

YAO
Just curious. Does it take you a while to warm up?

ELLIE
Again, don't know what I'm comparing it to, but I'm warm now.

YAO
Oh yeah?

ELLIE
Yeah.

YAO
Yeah?

ELLIE
Yeah.

YAO
You're turned on?

ELLIE
Are you?

YAO
Yes.

ELLIE
I am, too.

YAO
Do you like to talk?

ELLIE
Generally, or during sex? Ha. No. Not really. I don't mind, though.

YAO
You're gonna have to make some decisions. I don't know what to do with you.

ELLIE
You don't?

YAO
Just kidding. I do.

> *ELLIE and YAO move in for a kiss.*
>
> *Blackout.*

ELLIE
(*to the audience*) We're gonna take a fifteen-minute intermission.

ACT 2

SCENE 1

Lights up. ADINA *takes her place, centre stage.*

ADINA
(*to the audience*) I mean, I can tell the difference from when I was in grade one, two, three – then I couldn't tell, I mean, like, it doesn't matter then, whether you're a girl, a boy, a cat. Like, everyone will hang out with everyone. But, then, like, I think, like, starting even in grade five, there was a lot of, like, kind of like, picking your groups. And it was more like girls hung out with girls, and boys hung out with boys, and if you were a boy and you hung out with a girl, then that means you like the girl. Yeah, sometimes people like each other, but, like, people kind of make a big deal of it. Like, there are boys that like me but, like, honestly, they like every single girl. They just tell, like, their friends and every time that person walks by they start whispering to their friend about that person. Mostly boys are doing it to girls right now, but that will probably change just 'cause, we'll get older and, like, girls will, like, get more confident and, like, vocal about liking someone. Yeah, but it's quite annoying. But, also, like, like, my friends have a lot of boys that like them so when I'm with them that happens a lot. And mostly, like, it's awkward when it's you, but it's mostly funny when it happens to your friends. But, like, my friends at least, like, you don't make a big deal of it. Nothing honestly comes from it, grade six, so like, nothing. It's just like, acknowledging. Like, it's just awkward and then it stops, and some people would make a big deal of it, but like, it honestly just goes away. Like, the boy stops liking the girl and then he stops, like, doing it, like, eventually, thank God, it's so annoying. You know, 'cause they just, like, laugh and it's like, I wanna know what they're

saying, but you can't ask though, no, 'cause that would just make it more awkward. I think you just have to, like, just ignore it until it stops. Because eventually it will stop, you can't rush it.

SCENE 2

ELLIE
(*to the audience*) That was my sister, who is twelve. Now, we're going to show you an evening I had with two friends I've known since I was my sister's age, since twelve. One of them you've met already – the other unnamed orphan in *Annie*, Maria.

> ELLIE *and* MARIA *are walking through a field, approaching the University of Toronto Party with Consent event.*

MARIA
(*to ELLIE*) What are you learning from the playwriting? That loads of our friends like crazy shit? Are men or women crazier?

ELLIE
(*to MARIA*) I can't tell. They're talking to me, so... But loads of women are into crazy shit that might seem demeaning, like, to me, and I gotta wonder –

MARIA
– if you're a prude?

ELLIE
Yes, and if they like it really, like, because they have learned that from their former partners, internalized that expectation, right, but then does that even actually matter? If they want something, does it matter, like, what the origin of that is?

ELLIE and MARIA walk inside the doors. BRAD enters.

ELLIE
Is this it? Woah. Jesus. Everyone here looks like they're twelve. Right? Are we old?

MARIA
No! I'm still a student. What, are you saying I look older than these freshmen?

ELLIE
I am, sorry.

MARIA
Fuck you, man. I bring you to this thing, and you call me old.

BRAD
Hi, my name is Brad and I am here with Party with Consent. How is everyone?

The sound of cheering can be heard.

BRAD
Yeah – that's right! We're going to have a lot of fun today, people! Let me tell you a bit about myself: when I was eleven years old my father passed away in a car accident.

MARIA
Yeah, this is a real fun party so far.

ELLIE
(*laughing*) Shhh!

BRAD
I bring this up not to be a downer, but because it made me look at what masculinity meant, since I was without a male figure. And, um – it meant I developed a strong relationship with my mother...

BRAD adlibs quietly under the following lines.

ELLIE
Wait, I just realized a man is talking to us about this.

MARIA
Yeah?

ELLIE
No, it's fine, just interesting –

MARIA
Guys will listen to an older – attractive, if I may say – guy –

ELLIE
Don't sleep with sexual-consent Brad, or do, actually, and tell me about it for my play.

BRAD
(*adlibbing quietly until*)... Party with Consent. So, when you wanna ask someone out, it's a scary thing, right? Right?

Sound of the crowd responding.

BRAD
Right. So you're making yourself vulnerable doing so. That's why guys (who feel the burden to ask women out, and initiate) will sometimes find ways around asking directly. (*pointing to MARIA*) You! So, what might that be?

MARIA
Uh... Do you want to go for a walk?

BRAD
"Do you wanna go for a walk?" What else? That's right – or, even, "Do you want a drink?" "Do you wanna go back to my place?" The problem with that is, that can be misinterpreted. Everyone is at this school because they worked hard and are intelligent, committed students. But that doesn't mean you come at this with the same life experience. And that these phrases will have the same meaning. The only way to obtain real consent is to be transparent, is to ask what you're really asking, and then the only way to make sure consent is ongoing and enthusiastic, as it needs to be to be real consent, is to check in with your partner, after you've begun.

As BRAD speaks, the following words are projected onto a screen behind him:

CONSENSUAL INTIMACY REQUIRES:
· ENTHUSIASTIC CONSENT
ONGOING CONSENT
BOTH PARTNERS ABLE TO CONSENT

So, this can be awkward, right? By asking people out directly, we're opening ourselves up to the chance that they might say no. Which is scary. But what's scarier is the chance that if you aren't clear and direct when obtaining consent, that interaction could turn out to mean something very different to your partner. What do we need to do? How do we change this? Anyone?

A voice yells, "Ask!"

BRAD
Yes. Did everyone hear that? Be vulnerable, and ask someone out directly. They might say no. Hey, how many

students go to this school? Exactly. I'm here to tell you that you have way more power than you think you do. If someone hears that you asked someone out and they said no, it probably won't be as big a deal for them if they are turned down, and it might give them the courage to ask someone out – instead of using less-direct tactics to pursue someone, tactics that can become coercion. Don't let it fly if one of your friends is mistaking coercion for consent. If you see someone making the decision to go home with someone when they're too intoxicated to make that decision, to legally consent, speak up. It's a scary thing to do, yes, but everyone in this room has your back. We can be brave together. We're going to keep doing these things, and we're going to spread these messages, until the majority are showing up for the free condoms and snacks. You guys are the pioneers, so congratulations and thank you.

MARIA
(*to* ELLIE) I think I should let Brad know you coerced me into coming to this.

ELLIE
You wanted it.

MARIA
What now?

ELLIE
We take a condom from the bowl that says "Be Sure to Ask for Consent!" and get on with our lives?

MARIA
Yeah. I don't really see how this is helping, honestly. It feels like, just lip service, kind of. So when they're accused of turning a blind eye to on-campus rape, they can be like, "But, look – look at Brad and his PowerPoint presentation!" It's a nice thought, but –

ELLIE
Yeah. I know. God, I'm rather expecting that to be the feedback I get on this play.

MARIA
Hey, would it help your play for you to talk to a stripper?

ELLIE
Um, yeah.

MARIA
You're talking to one.

ELLIE
Really?

MARIA
Yup.

ELLIE
Seriously?

MARIA
Yup.

ELLIE
Cool. I really didn't see that coming – um, okay, tell all – how did this come about?

MARIA
Well, I was serving – everywhere, remember? I worked like, five or six places downtown in four years, and I had shitty male bosses. I always felt objectified and just like everyone's bitch so, like, kind of one day, jokingly, I thought, "I may as well be a stripper," and then... ha ha.

ELLIE
Did you know someone who got you into it?

MARIA
Nope. I tried it, originally it would just be for a week, whatever, and it turned out I liked it. Turned out it's honestly empowering. I get it, I'm asking to be looked at, I'm inviting people to. I'm expecting it and able to control it kind of because of that. It's not like I'm reading a book on the subway, and I look up and someone has their dick in their hand. This makes that stuff actually more bearable, weirdly, because if the world is full of disgusting men at least they're paying my rent. Also the place I work has strict rules – they're barely allowed to touch me and security is great at my place. I pick my clients, there is no backroom or anything, and I make great money – oh, and I make my own hours. I just work whenever I want and the bar doesn't take a cover of what I make. Some do, but I got lucky, yeah, I found a good place to try this. Yeah. I don't know if I would do it anywhere else, but – yeah. I don't tell people. So, don't say anything of course. It's definitely not for everyone.

ELLIE
Yeah, of course. Are you ever afraid someone you know will come in?

MARIA
Yup, you don't have hours you need to be on the floor though, so I'd just go sneak out the back. I have thought about that a lot, actually. It hasn't happened yet.

ELLIE
How long have you been –

MARIA
A year, coming up to.

ELLIE
And, what's the most significant observation –

MARIA
Yeah. This is what, like, why I brought it up – I remember when I first started, when I say you pick your clients, you go up to people and ask if they want to talk, basically. Which is a euphemism for a lap dance. But you do talk a bit at first, which is a way to screen people and to tell them the rules. If they're wasted and crossing boundaries at that point, grabbing at you, or whatever, I refuse them. Mostly I meet and work with really polite guys. Anyway, my first week, I was going up to people saying, "Hey, you wanna hang out?" or "You wanna go sit down with me?" whatever – and a bunch of men, like the first ten guys I asked said no. And they said it like, like I had just approached them at an Applebee's and asked if they wanted a lap dance, just like, "What the fuck is this girl doing?" So I went to a woman who'd worked there a couple years, she's our age but started young, and she let me suffer a while longer. I was fucking upset. I mean, it feels fucked up to be a stripper and asking people who've come into a strip club presumably for the purpose of meeting a stripper if they'd like to be stripped on and have them say no – not even that, but say no in such a – an indignant way, right? I'd never felt so unattractive – and I wanted to quit, so this lady, let's call her, um… I'm bad at this, what's a girl's name? Chelsea. Chelsea said to me, "Look around, it's not you, they're saying no to everyone. Some of these guys go to these clubs exactly to do that, to say no." And it's true. There are guys that will come, loads of them, and order drinks and say no all night to everyone who approaches them. Because, like, in their daily lives, they're pursuing women, and presumably it's not going too well if they're in a strip club, right, why not just go to a normal bar? And this is the only opportunity they may ever have to

feel the, um, empowerment they feel from declining female attention.

I think there's something to that. Let's steal a bunch of those condoms and leave. You can tell everyone here really wants to have sex tonight, and it's unnerving.

SCENE 3

About two hours later. ELLIE *and* MARIA *are on the subway after having gone for dinner.*

ELLIE
Okay – I feel drunk. How did that happen?

MARIA
We had wine at dinner.

ELLIE
Yeah, but also dinner. You're not drunk.

MARIA
I drink way more than you normally, and you kept up with me this time, champ.

ELLIE
I'm a champ.

MARIA
You are a champ. Also, you're an idiot and you don't eat bread –

ELLIE
That took a turn.

MARIA
You just had a salad. Classic.

ELLIE
Touché.

MARIA
Tired of your gluten-free bullshit, Moon! So yeah, that's why I need a drink still. Let's go to Bathurst. You can have water if you're down.

ELLIE
I'm down. I told Peter to meet us.

MARIA
What? Really? Why?

ELLIE
Because I haven't seen him since I got back from England.

MARIA
And he'll say good things for your play?

ELLIE
Maybe.

MARIA
He's an idiot. One that I will inevitably love until the day I die, but…

ELLIE
Yeah, me too.

MARIA
Remind me to tell you, I have a super-awkward Peter story for your play.

ELLIE
Oh, yay.

MARIA
Surely, though, you can get an honest guy's view from many sources, not just Peter.

ELLIE
Nah, any way I explain the project, I try to say as little as possible and definitely leave out the word "consent," 'cause, you know, that just puts it in a place in people's minds. (*pause*) But whatever I say, people deduce that I'm coming at it from a specific perspective, which is fair, but, yeah, guys just basically grin at me while I explain it, then say what they think I wanna hear. And I don't wanna freak myself out and actually go up to strangers. I should, though.

MARIA
You should. (*pointing out* SUBWAY MAN) Hey. He looks like a sexist – go talk to him.

ELLIE
He does.

MARIA
Do it. Why not? You're safe, 'cause I'm right here.

ELLIE
I seem drunk –

MARIA
No you don't.

ELLIE
Really?

MARIA
Really. Only I'd be able to tell.

ELLIE
I'm gonna do it.

MARIA
Do it!

ELLIE
This is art.

MARIA
Yup, it's art!

ELLIE approaches SUBWAY MAN.

ELLIE
Hi, excuse me, sir – I'm interviewing people I meet around Toronto about their experiences dating. Would you be up to talking for a few minutes?

SUBWAY MAN
It sounds a bit like you're asking me out.

ELLIE
Oh. I'm not.

SUBWAY MAN
You just want my dating history?

ELLIE
No, I want whatever you'll offer about your experiences navigating romance.

SUBWAY MAN
What is this for?

ELLIE
Basically I'm looking at where we're at – I'm writing a play – but this is the research, right now. It's gonna be about, like, how we decide we're interested in someone or someone's interested in us and how we communicate that.

SUBWAY MAN
So, like, consent?

ELLIE
Sure, right. That's right. So, as a man, what's your perspective on the expectations for men or women in the dating scene?

SUBWAY MAN
What, you mean – oh I think I know what you're getting at – 'cause like, women were oppressed and now it's like they're not, but we still have some things leftover from that time, right?

ELLIE
Right! So, what's that – how does that inform how you deal with women?

SUBWAY MAN
Well, fuck this. Honestly. You kidding me? You came up to me and asked me to talk into a recording about personal things – do you think you're oppressed? Would an oppressed woman do that?

ELLIE
I never said I was – and I'm a bit drunk, I'm so sorry –

SUBWAY MAN
Yeah, see? You're a bit drunk and you're up here bothering me. Imagine if the roles were reversed?

ELLIE
I asked, and – yeah. I'll go. So sorry.

SUBWAY MAN
It's okay. You don't –

ELLIE
No? Okay? Okay. (*pause*) So you feel that you have to walk a line? I don't wanna put words into your mouth.

SUBWAY MAN
HA! That's really fucking funny, 'cause, yes, yes you do wanna do just that. Well. I don't wanna talk to you anymore, thank you. I don't wanna put anything in your mouth, by the way.

ELLIE
I'm gonna go sit down now.

SUBWAY MAN
You're not attractive, by the way.

ELLIE
Cheers. (*to Maria*) Can we get off here?

MARIA
Of course. You are attractive, by the way.

ELLIE
I just don't wanna stay on this train.

MARIA
That's okay.

ELLIE
Which is stupid, 'cause I went up to him, and now I'm slinking off like I'm some victim here.

MARIA
Peter is gonna meet us closer to here anyway.

ELLIE
Is he?

MARIA
When I tell him to he will, yes.

SCENE 4

> PETER *is having a drink and talking to* ELLIE *and* MARIA.

PETER
When the Jian thing first came out I was terrified. And I'm still terrified, honestly. Because, well, I think I have usually been the more enthusiastic one in my experiences with women, and men, for that matter. And now I'm replaying every encounter I've ever had, shot by shot, just… terrified, that I missed a signal. That she, or he, but come on, more likely she, um, stopped being into it, and I was too into it to tell. What I mean here is that men have this pressure of being expected to initiate but not coerce. But then initiation can easily turn into coercion, it's a fine line. And if it does, I would be so absolutely horrified to find out that someone wanted to stop while they were with me, and didn't feel they could ask me to. I don't want to be with someone who doesn't want to be there. But I know that women feel that way, like they can't say no, often, because of conversations I've had with you and other girls I'm friends with, and I just never really want to ever have sex again in my life when I think about that shit. My ex, I've thrown her around and I thought those things were, you know, masculine, appealing to women. I don't see myself as threatening, but am I, just by virtue of having a penis? And now I'm terrified there's something out there that I've done. Yeah. You won't use my real name for this, right?

ELLIE
No, no. Of course not.

PETER
Good. I'm so paranoid about this. And I don't even smoke weed all the time anymore. I have to go, actually. You ladies kept me out way later than I was planning. Exhausting topic, too.

ELLIE
So amazing seeing you, Peter. Thank you for talking to me about this.

ELLIE, MARIA, and PETER all get up to hug.

PETER
Of course. So glad you're back now.

MARIA
Right?

ELLIE
You're the best.

MARIA
Bye, man.

PETER
Bye!

ELLIE
Bye!

MARIA
Bye.

PETER exits.

MARIA
Ah.

ELLIE
Ah. That was good, huh? He obviously went on forever, but I'll cut it down and be able to use lots of it – and it was also nice to see him.

MARIA
Yes, right. Oh, Peter. I wasn't expecting all that.

ELLIE
Yeah. He's growing up, maybe.

MARIA
Mmm.

ELLIE
Also, wait – what is your awkward Peter story? I figured asking about the Peter story in Peter's presence wasn't a good idea, but, it was killing me the whole time. Oh my God, what?

MARIA
Yeah, Jesus, I'm glad you didn't – bring it up, ha, God, yeah, good intuition. (*pause*) Ah. It's so awkward. I don't even know if I should – you're going to think it's so fucked.

ELLIE
What?

MARIA
Okay. The Peter story. Yeah, hearing him say all that just now was icing on top – yeah, okay, I'll give you the deets, whatever you want.

ELLIE
No, it's whatever you want –

MARIA
Okay. Okay. Well, Peter's interview just now is icing on the cake.

ELLIE
Wait? What cake?

MARIA
So, I'll give you the cake then.

ELLIE
Okay, give me the cake.

MARIA
I'll give you a mini cake.

ELLIE
A cupcake?

MARIA
This is like a personal cake.

ELLIE
That's a cupcake!

MARIA
Like, personal pizzas!

ELLIE
Still a cupcake!

MARIA
Okay. No, a personal cake is three cupcakes. Okay. Okay. Okay. Okay. So, I'm in bed with him after that night, the last Saturday before Christmas when all of us went out, you were in Montréal, I'm in his bed, because that's where I was

gonna sleep. And it's Peter, so obviously nothing is going to happen. Except, fuck, ha –

ELLIE
What? What?

MARIA
Yeah, we flirted and we teased each other and –

ELLIE
What? Peter? Weird.

MARIA
Yeah, I don't know, I was drunk, so I was into it, and we got a little too teasy for sure, because we were both drunk. But then we fell asleep. And Peter said to me, um, he was like, "I'm not gonna let you sleep with me, you're wasted, you're in a relationship, I won't let you do anything you regret, but I am gonna tease you." And I said, okay, if you promise, then I'll do the same. And we were… teasing each other all night, and it was fun. And we didn't do anything. So we were touchy but not touching – and I was just laughing the whole time, 'cause it was like, "Ha ha, you can't have me." And then I woke up, middle of the night, whatever time it was, and I woke up and he was pushing my head down, into his dick and – like, making me give him a blow job.

ELLIE
Woah. Peter?

MARIA
Yeah.

ELLIE
What. Really?

MARIA
Yeah. And then he rolled over on top of me and even said this, so I know he was awake and conscious, and he said, "This is for me now," and then he just inserted. And did it twice. And then came out. And then went back to sleep.

ELLIE
What? Maria, he raped you.

MARIA
Just in and in – two or three times and then held it and out and then – yeah. He didn't cum or anything.

ELLIE
But he raped you.

MARIA
Yeah, he basically raped me.

ELLIE
No, not "basically" – he raped you. Oh God, I'm so, so sorry that this happened to you.

MARIA
My only argument – and not in his favour, this is in my defence –

ELLIE
Sorry, I'm confused, why do you need a defence?

MARIA
No, because I slept in his bed and I teased him but, no, the only defence here is because I didn't know that happened to begin with. So he's inside, and I realize it's happening, and it feels super good, and I'm super confused. 'Cause I'm drunk, so I'm just going, "This feels really great 'cause I'm horny," and then it's like – "Oh, shit, you're not allowed to do that."

(*pause*) So I thought I'd cheated on Tyler until right now, basically. Because, yeah, it was him. I didn't say yes. I didn't say no. I don't know, really, what this means. Maybe I'm just making an excuse for myself, so that I didn't really cheat. I don't know. I never, ever considered that it was rape, until you just said that. Also the next morning, like, we had a nice morning, played video games, made lunch.

ELLIE
Fuck. I'm fucking so sorry about this.

MARIA
It's fine.

ELLIE
No, it's really not. What the fuck? Why did we just hang out with him? I'm so sorry, you didn't want to. I wasn't listening.

MARIA
Oh, no, look, whatever, I didn't speak up. He's my friend too, whatever. Like, he's a good guy. There's no reason to not be friendly or hang out in a group. I just wouldn't sleep at his again. Or hang out with him one-on-one.

ELLIE
No man, fuck, everything he said is gross and horrible now.

MARIA
No man, he made some great points. He just has no intuition.

ELLIE
Weren't you thinking, "What about the time you raped me?" the whole time? I can't believe we had that conversation with you sitting there –

MARIA
He probably doesn't remember. He was wasted. Yeah. Fuck. Whatever. (*pause*) It won't happen again is all that matters.

ELLIE
To you. Sorry. Sorry. I'm sorry – but, come on, it's not about intuition if you were sleeping. The way you described it, it isn't intuition.

MARIA
Who knows? I don't even know, I told my sister at Christmas, and it sounded way less sad and just more... awkward. I don't know, it might just be me having "rape" in my head now from hanging out with you.

SCENE 5

ELLIE

(*to the audience*) It took our friendship a few weeks to recover after this. But it did recover. I'm still friends with both of these people, Peter and Maria, and they're still friends with each other. They've had a conversation about this incident that Maria describes, but I cannot give you access to that conversation. This device (*motioning her phone*) gave me access to a lot, but with limits, and that's one of them. What I can give you access to is a conversation I had with Maria sometime later. This is going to be the last interview of the play.

MARIA and ELLIE are at Ellie's apartment.

MARIA

(*to ELLIE*) Okay, okay – where's your phone? I'm gonna ask you questions now. Aha! This is cool, I have the power now.

ELLIE

(*to MARIA*) Oh my God. That's what you thi–

MARIA

See?! It's annoying, right? So, how has this play made you see things differently – no, no, that's actually not what I wanna ask you, I wanna ask you about Jack.

ELLIE

Fuck off.

MARIA

No, what? I won't fuck off, because this is part of it, so it needs to be in here.

ELLIE
Wow.

MARIA
Jack, the forearm choker. You said you were having sex, and his forearm came down on your throat. Yeah?

ELLIE
Yes, as we've discussed.

MARIA
What? I'm trying to help you for your play. I just think it should be on record again and such so you can put it in, if you so deci–

ELLIE
Yes, fine, and I said, yes, that's what happened.

MARIA
Okay. (*pause*) Did you push him off or anything?

ELLIE
Um, no.

MARIA
Did you pass out?

ELLIE
No! God, no, not even close. Jesus. I just, like, couldn't breathe for a second, yeah, ha ha, and I, like, was panting, and then I felt embarrassed and, like, exposed, panting, and so I tried to do so discreetly and, like – blend it into sex noises.

MARIA
Can you demonstrate that, please?

ELLIE
Fuck off, no, I'm not going to demonstrate –

MARIA
I just think it would really help your play. And, excuse me, aren't you an actor?

ELLIE
Oh fuck, I am an actor. Okay, okay, it was like –

ELLIE makes an attempt at it and ends up just laughing.

MARIA
You're such a bad actor. That was – okay. You didn't say anything to him after?

ELLIE
Nope. Oh, here's maybe an opportunity for some better acting, because he kind of gave me this kind of smile at the end of the sex, this smile, like this.

ELLIE demonstrates a very stiff, closed-mouth smile, which hardly looks like a smile.

MARIA
That's not a smile –

ELLIE
No, like, I think it might have been, like, an acknowledgment. But yes, I might be, like, I am probably just projecting onto that.

MARIA
Okay. And then? Oh, wait – what happened then, Ellie Moon?

ELLIE
You're a horrible person.

MARIA
Fine, I'll say it: he cried! And when you told me off the record I said, "WHAT THE FUCK?"

ELLIE
That's good acting, that's exactly what you sounded like.

MARIA
Why did he cry?

ELLIE
We'd both been drinking, we were drunk. So the, that def contributed. He... was saying how hard it is to be 6'4" and be the first person that people see when they walk into a room, and his wanting to hide from that –

MARIA
(*mockingly*) Aww. Is this that part of the play where we get some violins?

ELLIE
Shhhhh, hey! Come on. Being tall is hard –

MARIA
Yeah, for men especially, the stigma against tall men –

ELLIE
Shhhhh, no – no, then about his ex who, his words, "abused" him –

MARIA
She must have been huge!

ELLIE
Emotionally! Which I believe, actually. And that prompted the crying. But like I say, I'm sure that he'd been drinking –

MARIA
Okay, okay, I'm a horrible person –

ELLIE
– No, you're not –

MARIA
– What did you do when he cried?

ELLIE
Um, I tried to be a good friend. I told him good things about himself, I forget exactly what, I cuddled him –

MARIA
God.

ELLIE
– I knew you were gonna say that.

MARIA
Okay. And then?

ELLIE
Oh, then he left. The end.

MARIA
No. So, okay, so then after the fact, what were things like between you?

ELLIE
Um. Yeah, he got weird around me for a while – a few months. I think it was the tears rather than the choking.

MARIA
At the time, did you tell anyone?

ELLIE
No.

MARIA
When did you first tell someone?

ELLIE
You, I told you – !

MARIA
Aw, I didn't know I was first – aw, thanks, what changed?

ELLIE
The Ghomeshi story broke.

MARIA
Oh, right.

ELLIE
Yeah. And I realized this was a thing. I didn't even think it was a thing before that. I thought it was weird, but, not, um, criminal.

MARIA
And then the Ghomeshi story broke, and you thought it might be criminal?

ELLIE
Yeah, it crossed my mind.

MARIA
And now do you think it was criminal?

ELLIE
No, no. I'm not comfortable calling it criminal now, no.

MARIA
Why not? Were you traumatized by it?

ELLIE
No, God no, certainly not. He was the one who was weird around me for a while, that was the worst part. I went, like, out my way to get him to see it was cool, then he got that it was cool, and we became friends again.

MARIA
But never had sex again?

ELLIE
No, no, not even close.

MARIA
Yeah. Why'd you stay friends?

ELLIE
Um, I think he's a clever, thoughtful, hilarious person. I like him.

MARIA
Are you still friends with him now that you're done school, though?

ELLIE
Ah, yup.

MARIA
When's the last time you spoke?

ELLIE
Um. A few months ago. I interviewed him for this piece.

MARIA
What did he say?

ELLIE
Um, inauthentic, guarded, politically correct shit. Couldn't use any of it.

MARIA
Did he figure out that he is a subject of this project beyond his own interview?

ELLIE
No, no.

MARIA
No?

ELLIE
Trust me. Definitely not. If I were to say –

MARIA
Yeah, if you were to say, "Remember how this happened?" What would he say?

ELLIE
Yeah, I think he'd be perplexed and say, "Uh, no"? I mean, I really would never ever bring it up. He'd get weird around me again, not worth it.

MARIA
If you found out that "Jack" – that you were part of, for him, like, a larger pattern of this kind of behaviour of his… if you found out he did this forearm choking thing to other people, without discussing it or asking, would you feel it was criminal?

ELLIE
Um, probably I would, yeah.

MARIA
So, in that case, would you come forward and report your experiences with, what are we calling him, "Jack"?

ELLIE
Yeah, "Jack." Um, no.

MARIA
No?

ELLIE
No.

MARIA
Do you think he's done this to other people?

Beat.

ELLIE
Probably, yeah.

MARIA
But *you* wouldn't come forward, not if a bunch of people stood up and said this happened to them non-consensually, not to back them up?

ELLIE
No.

MARIA
Really?

ELLIE
No.

MARIA

Yeah, okay. And you would never even just, like, bring it up with him –

ELLIE

No. Sorry but, as I said, no.

MARIA

Okay. Okay. And "No means no." Ha ha, agh, sorry – that's in bad taste. Sorry. Sorry, this just got, I'm just, uncomfortable.

ELLIE

No, it's okay. I am too.

MARIA

I guess we can leave it at that.

ELLIE

(*to the audience*) That used to be the end, but now this is the end. (*pause*) When I put out the Facebook request for interview subjects, I had an agenda. I wanted to know why I tolerated pain or discomfort during sex. Is it lack of respect for myself, lack of connection with myself, or have I just not had enough sex, and is that part of it? How do you maintain control while making discoveries? What does any of this say about me, about us? What does sex give access to, what can communicating give access to – what's the cost of that access? (*pause*) That's it. Thanks for coming.

THE END

NOTE

Scene one of this play quotes Jian Ghomeshi's October 26, 2014, Facebook post, written the day of his firing by the CBC. This post has been removed from Facebook, but was widely reported, and can still be found in its entirety at globalnews.ca/news/1637310/full-text-jian-ghomeshis-post-on-why-he-believes-cbc-fired-him/.

WHAT I CALL HER

PRODUCTION HISTORY

What I Call Her was first produced from November 16 to December 8, 2018, by In Association and Crow's Theatre in Toronto, Ontario, with the following cast and crew:

KATE	Charlie Gould
KYLE	Michael Ayres
RUBY	Ellie Ellwand
Director	Sarah Kitz
Production Manager	Suzie Balogh
Stage Manager	Ashley Ireland
Producer	Annie Clarke
Lighting Designer	Imogen Wilson
Composer and Sound Designer	Ali Berkok
Fight Director	Bailey Green

CHARACTERS

KATE, age twenty-five, female
KYLE, age twenty-five, male, Kate's live-in partner
RUBY, age twenty, female, Kate's sister

SETTING

The one-bedroom apartment in the Leslieville neighbourhood of Toronto that Kate and Kyle have shared for just over eighteen months.

TIME

One winter evening in 2018, with the action unfolding in real time.

NOTE

A slash / indicates overlapping dialogue. A beat maintains the rhythm and shouldn't be held for too long. A silence is longer than a beat, and can end at the actors' discretion.

TOP: Michael Ayres and Charlie Gould in *What I Call Her* at Crow's Theatre, Toronto, Ontario (November 16 to December 8, 2018).
Photo by Dahlia Katz. Reproduced with permission.

BOTTOM: Ellie Ellwand in *What I Call Her* at Crow's Theatre, Toronto, Ontario (November 16 to December 8, 2018).
Photo by Dahlia Katz. Reproduced with permission.

WHAT I CALL HER

> KATE and KYLE sit on their couch. The furniture in their place doesn't match – it looks nice, for an apartment inhabited by two twenty-five-year-olds. They've done what they can with donations and trades; there is attention to detail and care, but just not many resources.

KATE
I feel scared.

KYLE
Why? I mean – do you want a drink?

KATE
Yeah.

KYLE
Yeah.

> KYLE goes off to get her a drink. KATE is alone. KYLE can still hear KATE, though; the place is small.

KATE
But I shouldn't say "feel." It's not a feeling, it's a sensation.

> KYLE returns with two glasses of wine and gives one to KATE.

KATE
Right?

KYLE
Yup.

KATE
Just, the wintertime, yeah... Strong.

KYLE
The feeling?

KATE
The sensation, but no, I meant the wine, I don't like sweet wine, as you know, but this –

KYLE
Is expensive from work, stole it, exhibit opening.

KATE
Nice. How do I change a sensation? My thoughts will follow. The two together are a feeling, y'know, that's right – right?

KYLE
Yeah.

KATE
How do I change the sensation?

KYLE
I could roll a jay?

KATE
Not right now.

KYLE
Okay, cool. We could have sex?

KATE
Nah.

KYLE
Okay, cool.

KATE
I just wanna sit.

Beat.

Did you read? The thing? I sent it to you? On Facebook, about, yeah, those siblings when their, I think it was their dad, when he passed, they put out an obituary, and it got published in an American paper... okay, oh man, let me find it.

KYLE
Okay.

Beat. KATE pulls out her phone.

KYLE
I think I got the gist, though.

KATE
(*searching on her phone*) Where is it?

KYLE
The scathing obituary, yeah, you told me.

KATE
Yes! I – No! I – I can't, fuck, I can't find it.

KYLE
I don't need to –

KATE

Can you check your phone? Why? Why not?

KYLE

I get message notifications from Facebook, I don't – I got the idea, he had some, like, financial-criminal stuff, money laundering, stole from his kids too, left them nothing, and his kids outed him for that in their obituary, that's all it is, right?

KATE

Yeah, but it's well written –

KYLE

I get it, I don't need to –

KATE

Why?!

KYLE

Because I find it sad, that's why.

KATE

Oh. I know, I know, babe. It's also beautiful, though.

KYLE

I guess. I feel so lucky. My parents are so nice – I have to call them soon.

KATE

I'm so happy for you, babe. Sincerely. Does that sound strained? Yup. It shouldn't though, 'cause I mean it. It's part of my getting woke around this shit, being happy for people who had what I didn't. Fuck, I sound like an asshole.

KYLE

A bit. Sorry, was I allowed to admit that –

KATE
Yes, you don't have to ask what you're allowed –

KYLE
Sorry.

KATE
You don't have to apologize!

>   *Beat.*

KYLE
Would you ever put out an obituary like that? For your mom? A scathing obituary, about your mom?

KATE
No. Maybe. No. I'd get sued.

KYLE
By – her husband?

KATE
Yeah, piece of fuckin', yeah – also, my sister.

KYLE
Oh, yeah, fair.

KATE
Is it?

KYLE
I mean fair that you would worry about that. Not that she'd sue you.

KATE
Yeah. She's had a different experience of her.

KYLE
Yeah.

KATE
Just, we are five years apart in age –

KYLE
Yeah –

KATE
Timing, ugh –

KYLE
Totally.

KATE
Maybe I'd write something on Facebook, though.

KYLE
About?

KATE
About my own parental-abuse situation. (*pause*) Like, like my own obituary for her. If it's on my own Facebook page, it's my right, right? I mean, the one I read, that was printed in a newspaper – fucking brilliant. I couldn't do that, not while my sister's alive.

KYLE
And she'll outlive you...

KATE
Hey! –

KYLE
Ruby is five years younger, and I see that girl's Instagram, must be at least almost paleo at this point. You smoke.

KATE
Weed!

KYLE
It's still bad for your lungs, you don't even vape –

KATE
It dilates your lungs, so actually, that's not all bad –

KYLE
That's you on some of your latest bullshit.

KATE
Hey.

KYLE
Sorry.

KATE
It's fine.

Beat. KATE *returns to her phone.*

KATE
I found the article! Fuck Messenger. Okay... where is... Oh, this is what I wanted to read you: when asked their reasons for putting out the obit, they said,... "We wanted people to think about their own greed and to ask themselves: 'do you want this to be your legacy? Do you want this to be your obituary?'"

KYLE
No.

KATE
It was a rhetorical question, babe, this would never be your obit.

KYLE
Hey. Do you still want?

KATE
What?

KYLE
Babies? I'm a dad on the prowl.

KATE
Yeah, I know.

KYLE
That's all right to say, right?

KATE
Borderline, but yeah.

KYLE
You still want, yeah?

KATE
Yeah. No time soon... eventually.

KYLE
Course, yeah.

KATE
Yeah, jeez, let my own mom die first. (*pause*) Yeah. So. (*pause*) Like, at least another week or two. (*pause*) But really, like, talking for kids, like, ten years, actually. That's when we'll own property, realistically. Not sooner.

KYLE
Unless a market crash happens.

KATE
It won't.

KYLE
A week or two. Okay. What else did Ruby say?

KATE
No, this was from Woody this time – her husband – yeah, my "stepdad, Woody."

KYLE
Chilling.

KATE
Yeah, I've only met him that one time but yeah, he seemed to live up to the expectations around that name – he sent a picture, she looks like shit. Like they do in movies about cancer deaths – *My Sister's Keeper*, Abigail Breslin –

KYLE
She doesn't play the cancer sister, though, she plays her keeper –

KATE
Her sister's keeper, yeah, anyway, I just mean she's in it, anyway, I just mean, bald and very white and skinny – I don't mean thin, she's not, she doesn't look that thin, I mean like, her skin, there is more of it. Skin... ny.

KYLE
Less hair. No hair.

KATE
Maybe that's it, yes.

KYLE
I remember when my uncle Paul died, leukemia, yeah, they sort of look like Pillsbury people.

KATE
Sure.

KYLE
He was a good man though, of course, so I kind of like thinking of him that way, like a benevolent Pillsbury person just binging on baked goods. He cared so much for others in his life, in a way I'm glad he got to be ill and to be cared for, I think he surrendered to it and, like, liked it, ultimately, but I don't really know, he stopped communicating pretty early. So, it's all just what we wanna make of it. I guess I'm ever the optimist: I think dying was nice for him.

Beat.

I just got your Facebook message now. Fuck Messenger.

KATE
I feel a bit bad for Woody.

KYLE
Yeah? Man. Dear sweet uncle Paul.

KATE
I don't know.

KYLE
Hmm? Sorry.

KATE
Yeah. I guess it's hard to talk to you about, like, the messages I get from, from, from my sister, from Ruby, when you and your sisters – you know, it feels like my failing, when I know

it's not, 'cause, like, she's been brainwashed and I was a kid, those weren't fights my mom and I got into, that was abuse. But God, unlike those people that posted that obit, they did it together, they had each other – Ruby is so much younger –

KYLE
And had a different experience, yeah.

> *Beat.*

It's not the same, but, like, my sisters hate my dad.

KATE
Do they?

KYLE
Yeah, well, not hate – but they resent him. They think he hit on their friends.

KATE
Aw, what?! That's a big deal.

KYLE
I don't mean, like, he raped them, just that he was like…

KATE
Yeah… That's a big deal…

KYLE
Yeah, they think so, too.

KATE
You get along great with your dad…

KYLE
Yeah, well –

KATE
You do.

KYLE
We do, I really like the guy – he obviously never did it with my friends, I had, like, no female friends.

KATE
Maybe that's why.

KYLE
No, no, I was a loser – I thought any girl who looked at me wanted to fuck me, and they didn't, of course. So, I never had that experience with my dad is my point, different siblings in the same family –

KATE
No, woah, no, you don't get to say, "Well, I'm a white man and he never hurt me."

Optional line, depending on casting:

KYLE
I'm not a white man.

KATE
You know what I mean.

KYLE
People aren't just bad or good.

KATE
Yeah.

KYLE
You don't think she's all good or bad either, I've heard you say it.

KATE
Sure, I'm able to hold many different complex ideas in my mind. I know no one is bad. I also know she made me feel a frozen kind of fear in my bones when I was very little. And you know, loud movies or TV give me that again and wintertime and when she dies, God, like, next week, oh my God, maybe, right? It will? Stop? (*pause*) And the Facebook thing. Maybe. Isn't it, too, a way to go and say, "Hey, community, I come from this history, I'm at risk of carrying on the cycle of abuse, please, this is my thing, look out for me."

KYLE
You want to be taken care of.

KATE
No! Fuck, stop, no. (*pause*) I mean, maybe. But I just want to be held accountable. Everything's possible, if – I'm, I'm twenty-five. I could do anything. I feel, like, full-elated drunk saying this. I'm not drunk. I'm being stupid. (*pause*) What if I wrote it and posted it? Really?

KYLE
Honestly? I think it's vengeful and, um, self-centred, and doesn't respect how other people who knew your mom will want to grieve and remember her –

KATE
Okay, okay. (*pause*) I know, I'm getting, like, high just on the feeling of, like, not being quiet.

KYLE
Her life and legacy don't totally belong to you.

Beat.

KATE
Yeah. (*pause*) Everything's vengeful if someone's paying attention. (*pause*) No, but yeah, no, I won't post it. I'll just write it and not post it.

Beat.

I can be, y'know, irritable, when, like, you know. Loud movies, but also other times, as you know. Right, I can be so, unreasonable and am I just, like, what do you think, trying to get absolved with this abuse stuff? I do, y'know, I remember things that were definitely abuse, so this is what, but like, I am hyperbolic, and imaginative, and I can remember things wrong – and build stories to, like, excuse myself. You know this. And I've always, right, explained this behaviour of mine to you as, like, a thing I do because I have this history of abuse.

KYLE
Not always. And you can also be just fucking great.

KATE
Aw, thanks babe. But no, I decided my past, like, affected me more than I realized but... like, I don't know, what if my fucking awful behaviour is just a thing I do not attributed to any trauma, and the real history is actually just the history of me doing this thing, being crazy, and blaming others for my being crazy.

KYLE
Crazy people don't ask if they're crazy.

KATE
Oh, I think they must sometimes.

Beat.

I won't post it, that would be crazy. (*pause*) I have things to work on in myself. I am working on them away from people that hurt me. I have to let that ... be – also! Noticing it is the first step.

KYLE
Yes.

KATE
Yes! So, if I am crazy, at least I've noticed. And I'm closer then to not being crazy. But, what's the next step? It's living in a world where I can do the work I have to do in plain sight of others who could help. What?

KYLE
Nothing, no. I just, you want to write and post a scathing obituary, ha, you do, I know you're going to. I just can tell you're going to –

KATE
Don't do that "I know you're going to do this shit," that's bullshit. It traps someone. I used to do it to myself, expect myself to do the worst thing, I'd be her right now if I still – and "scathing," really? We're talking about recounting historical facts that I lived through, in my life, as a child, without any say in the matter. Do you see like, five-, six-year-olds regularly, do you stand beside them and see how fucking tiny they are, how relatively powerless and defenceless and innocent, and how even their worst behaviours are like, "That's a six-year-old"? I was a six-year-old.

KYLE
You rarely go into detail.

KATE

Yeah. I didn't know that your dad creeped on your sisters' friends and your sisters don't like him.

KYLE

You don't always ask.

Beat.

KATE

I'm jealous that you and your sisters can disagree on some history, I don't get that with my sister. Ruby is furious with me. Ruby will be whether or not I post this for not going to see her in hospice, if I'd gone to see her, Ruby would be mad at me for not seeing her more while she's been sick, before she went to hospice. If I'd seen her more while she'd been sick, Ruby woulda been mad at me for not seeing her before she got sick. You don't get vilified for your perspective on your dad – which is, like, a bit of a denial of theirs, of your sisters' experiences, right? To be like, he never hurt *me*.

KYLE

I don't deny he did that to their friends, though. Like, your sister doesn't even think you were abused, right?

Beat.

KATE

I guess – I would, I don't know, I wouldn't be happy if I were them: your sisters. Maybe I'm just a bitch who needs to alienate everyone. I do wanna post that shit on Facebook. It might make everyone, and you included, hate me. But fuck, it also will set me free.

KYLE

I will never hate you, babe.

KATE

I won't post it. But writing it will free me: free speech is the antidote to shame.

KYLE

Free to do what?

KATE

I don't know, that's not how free speech works. You just let your speech be free and let it be what it will be, with free speech. It's not free to be anything, just free. That's what free means.

KYLE

How free will you feel, though, if you're shamed for this. Are you really prepared for that?

KATE

I'm talking about writing it, not posting it! Listen, please. Do you think she deserves the shaming obituary?

KYLE

I think so, but I can't know.

KATE

The last time we spoke on the phone, she urged me to kill myself –

KYLE

I know –

KATE

So then you can't know what? She included my short story –

KYLE

I know –

KATE

Being published! In her email newsletter! I got emails from people I hadn't seen since I was a kid, saying they read the story, because she told them in their letter –

KYLE

I know –

KATE

We hadn't spoken in over four years, our last conversation she urged me to kill myself, and she gets to cite my achievements as though they belong to her? As though I do? Do you understand? I cannot have her die and then have dozens of conversations where I nod politely at the suggestion that she was, you know, spirited and "out there" and a strong personality but good and loving. She used to hurt me very seriously, with knives and forks and her fist, like big time, when I was like, four, five, through till, like, eleven.

KYLE

I know –

KATE

I had very little choice in all of this!!

KYLE

Yes! I know!! Okay, I get it. You're right. (*pause*) So why do you need to write one single, like, blanket post about this? Even not to post, even as an exercise? Why is that even – what does it? What if, you, you just *know* this stuff and the conversations you have with every mourner, you make them honest and calm, what if you told every mourner that or some version of that, engaged in a conversation, on a case-by-case –

KATE
'Cause –

KYLE
And your relationship to her death, to your grief, God, it will change and keep changing, you don't need to make one decision now about how –

KATE
No, **NO** grief – the pain is not that, it's like, like, equally painful to the abuse, right, is the understanding of it that I've carried, right, that I share responsibility with her for these things that happened, that it's just a difficult mother, daughter – an understanding reinforced by a culture unable to accept a white woman as threatening and dangerous to their child's safety – this, listen! It took me starting to babysit at the end of high school and realizing that if one of those children was seriously hurt because of a physical confrontation between us, oh, that would be on me, obviously, and me alone. I just, I know, I know that had I had the same experiences with my male or my non-white parent, I would not have had to fight against my sense of culpability –

KYLE
Oh fuck off, you've already started writing the post. I can tell. You're not even! You're just writing the – you probably want it to go viral, don't you – fuck!

KATE
I'm not posting it!! So I'm not going viral!! Stop. Fuck! And that's fucking dismissive. I just said a lot of ideas, but the fact that I have them and want to share them is more, like, worthy of note, or comment, than what those ideas are. Women are such calculating bitches, huh? Whenever we nail it, it's like, "Why did they want to nail it? Very

disconcerting." (*pause*) Are you worried how your parents will look at it?

KYLE
No, I'm not worried for me, or *my* life, babe.

KATE
Right.

> *Beat.*

KYLE
My parents love you. They don't always understand, right, like how much my mom just wanted you to join us for Christmas – the way she sees it is, we love you, so you should be with us. She doesn't get it.

KATE
Even though she's married to a creep?

KYLE
Don't call my dad a creep, please. (*pause*) I don't think we say nice things for people after they die for them, we do it for ourselves.

> *Beat.*

KATE
Tell me about your dad stuff. He's never been even slightly creepy with me, which is very interesting. I'm not saying I don't believe the experiences of your sisters' friends, obviously, I believe women. But like, does he just respect me as your property really hard? 'Cause that's sweet. I mean, or he doesn't find me attractive, but I doubt that, anyway, it's never about attractiveness with harassment. Power. So, I guess he wants to allow you some, over me, so sweet. I'm not being sarcastic, it is, kinda, eh?

Beat.

KYLE
Well. There is, you know, one thing you could consider: does posting the thing make it easier, or harder, for you to not then become your mother?

KATE
Easier. Because, if I do that – I need to understand my future possible daughter, could do that, to, like I am setting the rules – making a world where there are consequences. (*pause*) Imagine if she'd said, if she'd told some people, "I'm worried about my anger with my kid." I'll do that if I need to. Maybe she couldn't, or maybe she did. (*pause*) No, she definitely didn't. She's a coward.

KYLE
And people are bad with women asking for help.

KATE
And men.

KYLE
True. (*pause*) Not that it's the same.

Beat.

I went and had coffee with her.

KATE
Sorry? Who?

KYLE
Oh, no!

KATE
Her?! –

KYLE

God no, sorry – no, I mean Darcy, the girl, the *woman*, one of the women, that my sisters, they, um –

KATE

Shit! What?

KYLE

Yeah, y'know, they said I should talk to, for... clarity, with my dad –

KATE

They told you to do that? They connected you to someo– you didn't tell me any of this. Babe.

KYLE

Yeah. Sorry.

KATE

And?

KYLE

What? Oh, oh... Sorry. No. I don't know. I found it embarrassing.

KATE

What did this girl say?

KYLE

What kind of a mood are you in?

KATE

Pardon? Please don't treat me like I'm radioactive, that's the shit I find... I'm never really in a bad mood, until you suggest that I'm this undignified thing unable to control my reactions to things – I find that kind of thing very hard to control my reaction to.

KYLE
I understand.

KATE
You do it, though? Is it maybe like a control tactic? Even a subconscious one? You're smart, and you do it a lot.

KYLE
I'm sorry, I think it's allowed, I think, because you have a sense of humour about yourself.

KATE
Do I?

KYLE
Yeah? A desire to comment on your own psychology all the time, at least. You would say it if I didn't. I can stop. It's a reflex more than anything. 'Cause you'd say it if I didn't, so then I anticipate...

KATE
I guess so.

Beat.

KYLE
One thing my dad told me, about, like, when he had me, he said, 'cause he grew up with shitty parents, right, and he said that when he had a kid, me, he learned that a huge part of loving a kid is just accepting their love. 'Cause kids can feel it if you aren't open to it. I know, this from the guy who then hit on my sisters' friends.

KATE
Yeah, and so, to what degree? What did she say?

KYLE
She said, Darcy said... Just like, comments.

KATE
So, there wasn't any – ?

KYLE
Like? No. No, that I'm aware of, no. Darcy wasn't aware of anything like that either, she said. He also might have done worse and I might never know. That's so possible. I felt paranoid, like, what percentage of the truth was Darcy telling me? And what about women that weren't friends with his, ugh, like, he's certainly hardwired, to some degree, the comments, they are gross... Like, I like your jeans, about being a bad girl or good girl, ugh, and my sisters' friends, they felt uncomfortable, they, they cost some friendships, humiliated my sisters. How does the guy who, like, tells that story about accepting my love, and who was the dad that, like, begged me to play catch with him, I didn't even want to, how does he then have so little intuition and, or, like, well, humanity? Do you know? I know, I don't expect, I don't know.

KATE
I'm sorry. Fuck. I love you.

KYLE
I love you.

KATE
I know – I didn't even, know about your sisters until like, like, they always seemed cool with your dad, you never mentioned.

KYLE
Yeah, no, they've always, like, been steady on this being the truth but never, like, I don't know, wanted to hold it against him, or divide the –

KATE
The family, divide the family, yeah.

KYLE
Yeah. The whole "Me Too" thing definitely, like, made them, um, value their experience differently.

KATE
That's great.

KYLE
Yeah.

Beat.

KATE
I like your dad. (*pause*) We're living in a post-Weinstein world. (*pause*) I wasn't starved... by my mom, I didn't have cigarettes put out on me. I had food and a bed but... yeah... like, like, the Weinstein thing, like... the worst was just knowing it could always happen, to whatever degree. And her comments, like, hearing her explain to Ruby why she – ugh, I'm so sorry to keep talking about this – Have you talked to your sisters since talking to Darcy?

KYLE
No.

KATE
Okay.

Beat.

KATE
What happened at work?

KYLE
I booked some field trips. I had to walk through the new exhibit. It was nice.

KATE
Cool. That's the Egypt one?

KYLE
Yeah. (*pause*) I'll talk to my sisters at some point about it. After I figure out what to say, exactly. There's how I feel, and then there's what to say.

KATE
I never think of it like that.

> *Beat.*

At what point, my temper – ?

KYLE
Yeah.

KATE
Don't say "yeah" like you know what I'm talking about when I say "my temper." Actually, no. Do. Good. Yes, at what point, does excusing my temper and my need to put myself first seem reasonable, because of my... history... and when does that become excusing me for like – being, you know –

KYLE
You're not... her.

KATE
Thanks. Sorry, were you gonna say more?

KYLE
Um, no.

KATE
Cool. (*pause*) The idea of the scathing Facebook obituary, what if... I could do one that, ensured my dignity? And, like, attacking her dignity would not reflect well on mine, so hers too, ours – our dignity. Not that my dignity is tied to hers.

KYLE
My dignity is tied to my dad's.

KATE
Yeah. Well, he raised you and didn't hurt you or walk out on you.

KYLE
Yeah. I just, don't wanna be a creep when I grow up.

KATE
You're not a creep! Babe, you're so not a creep. I'm the creep.

KYLE
Thanks.

KATE
I promise, I'll always be the creep. (*pause*) Look at me: I promise.

> *Beat.*

I think I would just, sorry to bring this back to me, but I think I wanna just write it. I'm a writer, it'll make me feel better –

KYLE
The mean obituary?

KATE

Yeah. I won't post it. Obviously. She's not even dead yet. It's just for me.

KYLE

But won't you wanna really make it great, and then once it's great, won't you really wanna share it?

KATE

No. I won't even make it great.

KYLE

Hmm.

KATE

I won't! (*pause*) I want to say... a lot. Can you help me, though, actually?

KYLE

With what?

KATE

Words, ideas, bouncing ideas –

KYLE

Making it not great?

KATE

No, I won't post it! She's not even dead!

KYLE

After she dies you will.

KATE

It would give me something to look forward to. I'm kidding. I don't wanna kill my sister, remember. (*pause*) I don't wanna kill anyone. Believe it or not. (*pause*) I'm not a heartless bitch who wants to kill… anyone. (*pause*) Like, I didn't have an abortion because it was yours, eh, I had it 'cause I'm twenty-five.

KYLE

What? What are you? I know. Why would you say that? I don't think abortion is killing, or that you're heartless. I was just –

KATE

I know you wanna talk about it. What were you gonna say? You were just – ?

KYLE

Sad. I don't think you did anything wrong.

KATE

But I know it's like you had an abortion, too, I know.

KYLE

What is your fucking problem?

KATE

No problem. (*pause*) What? (*pause*) What. (*pause*) Have you seen shit from me that might make you call up Ruby and be like, "Fuck her – I'm with you."

KYLE

What?

KATE

Answer my question please.

KYLE

What was your question again?

KATE

Have you seen shit from me to make you think I might deserve this shit?

KYLE

What shit? Abuse? No.

KATE

No... My family hating me, I don't know.

KYLE

I don't know how to answer that. I'm on your side.

KATE

Okay. Yeah. Sorry. (*pause*) I wouldn't treat a child who needed me the way I treat you, sometimes. I need to stop treating you that way though. I'm sorry.

KYLE

It's okay.

KATE

Will you help me write this?

KYLE

Okay.

KATE

You'll help? Yeah? Wow. Okay. Wow this is going to feel good, which it's totally allowed to.

>   *Beat.*

I want to – okay... I'm gonna, just – can I use your laptop?

KYLE

Sure.

KATE
Can you grab it?

KYLE
Sure.

KYLE goes to get the laptop. KATE sits, thinking.

KATE
Well, how specific do I get with the abuse? I'll say it was physical, verbal, and emotional – all the abuses! Ha, no... no, not sexual abuse. Oh, but like, *she* was sexually abused as a child –

KYLE returns with laptop.

KYLE
Was she?

KATE
Yeah, you knew that, babe – her mom, too.

KYLE
Right, fuck.

KATE
Yeah. Didn't you? 'Cause that's what her organization, like, it's for children who've been victims of sexual abuse, because she –

KYLE
Oh yeah, of course, and she started it, 'cause she, yeah, I knew.

KATE
Yeah. The hypocrisy... Yeah, so, I wanna say – that seems... okay. I'm gonna write something and then read it to you,

probably in chunks. I'll probably want like, like, wording suggestions. I wanna be – yeah. Don't say no to anything outright, though. Be encouraging, say yes.

KYLE

That's how you say yes to some things, though, by saying no to other things.

KATE

Fine. What was her birthday again? Oh yeah... (*pause*) hmm... (*pause*) I wish I could write that she "died alone," like that one I sent you about the father who stole from his family, but my sister and stepdad are with her, so...

KYLE

You wish she was dying alone?

KATE

God no. Of course not. It just sounds good, I meant, ignore me, forget it. Sorry.

KYLE

I think everyone dies alone anyway.

KATE

Okay – where did she go to university? Oh yeah.

KYLE

Yeah, where did she go?

KATE

UVic.

KYLE

Nice, for?

KATE
English.

KYLE
Cool. That her only degree?

KATE
Teacher's college.

KYLE
Right, of course. Cool.

KATE
Shhh. Be quiet a sec, I gotta figure how I...

Long silence. KATE *types.*

KATE
Shit. It's turning out more complimentary than I intended. (*pause*) We're so, ugh, programmed to be nice.

KYLE
Can you read it to me?

KATE
It's not done, I just started, obvio–

KYLE
Yeah, read me what you have.

KATE
No, I'm not reading it aloud, that's embarrassing – sure, read it off, my, yeah...

KYLE
Okay.

KYLE reads the laptop screen over KATE's shoulder.

KYLE
It's not that complimentary. (*pause*) Why do you find it embarrassing?

KATE
I don't know.

Silence as KATE keeps writing.

KATE
I do want to, find a way to acknowledge how others, like, remember her, how she's been there for people that just… aren't me. (*pause*) How 'bout, "She is also survived by the young women she mentored in recent years as well as many short-lived but loving and intense friendships past"?

KYLE
Sure.

KATE
I'm gonna write that she was a childhood sexual abuse survivor.

Beat.

KATE
Ugh. This isn't as fun as I'd expected.

KYLE
Do you want a drink?

KATE
Yeah.

KYLE
Or to stop?

KATE
No. (*pause*) I think I maybe sabotaged, I mean, any reconciliation efforts at a certain point, like in high school, because, well, 'cause she made me feel I was betraying her by having other people I leaned on. And also, I think I thought I would get to trade her in, in effect – that I could get more access to other people if she wasn't there.

KYLE
Well, yeah, that sounds – from everything you've said about her, yeah, alienating you from other people who cared about you, guilting you for those relationships.

KATE
But I built up their importance, to yeah, like, probably heal myself – but she saw that and it hurt and I probably used it to hurt her. It's probably why she could never backpedal with me. She thinks I've told all the people in my life, lovers and mentors, people who've cared about me, what a monster she is.

KYLE
Well, you have.

KATE
Yeah. And that's my right. But did it cost me, has it? No. Just, it's just I remember, you know, I remember her rubbing my head once when I was maybe ten or eleven, that was... nice. (*pause*)

But... yeah, I remember it and, like, trying to will it not to stop, exactly because it was so, exceptional. Anyway. Just, I can't get another one. I don't think I got that till, yeah. Okay. Okay.

Beat.

KYLE
When I have kids, and I hope I do with you, I just want them to know they can do bad things without being bad people. I wish, I don't know, I want you to remember that, too. It sounds obvious – but. Come here. Let me rub your head, babe.

KATE
No, I gotta finish this. One sec. Love you.

KYLE
Love you.

Beat.

KATE
It's hard to consider the reality of, like, her feelings, because I, I don't know, had to prioritize my own feelings with her for the sake of my, you know, safety.

Beat.

You had an experience of the procedure I had this summer. An emotional reaction. And I didn't.

KYLE
And I don't judge you for that.

KATE
I know you don't. So I needed to let you be sad, and let you have an emotional reaction and support you, 'cause on this one thing, I'm fine. So I can be there for you, you know? Let me be. That's – yeah.

KYLE
I don't know what it's like to be, like, you know, able to have a baby – so yeah, no, it's not fair to you, it's selfish for me to, like, be sad, it's your body –

KATE
No it's not selfish, it's fair, fairness is never selfish.

KYLE
I don't…

>   *Beat.*

KATE
… Yeah?

>   *Silence.* KYLE *doesn't want to talk about this and looks on his phone.* KATE *goes back to typing.* KATE *types for a while.* KYLE *is still on his phone. A long silence.*

KYLE
So, I looked it up: did you know you can't legally defame the dead? So you couldn't get sued! Wow, people just, like, lose their rights after they die! That makes sense, I guess. There are a lot of people who have lived.

>   *Silence.* KATE *types for a while. Then she reads aloud.*

KATE
"She lived in a world where she felt enormous fear that she had to puff herself up to protect herself in and also a world where she was constantly punished for this, in a culture that fears and isolates angry women. Especially during her most significant periods of isolation, she was prone to violent fits of rage. Unfortunately, caring for young children was an

experience she found particularly isolating, especially her eldest child, to whom she became a mother to in a brand new country, without the support of extended family, so her children – and one of her children in particular, with whom she was still estranged when she died – were victims of her severe and, for a period of about seven years, regular physical and verbal attacks…" I know my sister would – it's just for me, no posting, remember?

KYLE
Yes.

KATE
There's more, that's just a small part, umm… "She very sadly lacked the capacity to self-reflect or take responsibility for her actions. She felt her own sense of victimhood acutely throughout her life and left this world denying any culpability for her abusive behaviour. She was typically overwhelmed by her own experiences and struggled to empathize with others and hear things that didn't align with her sense of reality. Much to her own great suffering, she cut herself off from anyone who challenged her and her account of things. She was a victim of our societal expectations for motherhood, of her own expectations for herself, her own fear and pride, of serious untreated borderline personality and bipolar disorders, as well as and likely as a result of the aforementioned conditions, periods of depression and substance abuse. She was a victim of a societal inability to understand women with rage as victims of abuse."

KYLE
It's good.

KATE
It's not that good.

KYLE

You should use her name though, not just "she."

KATE

Yeah, you know, I don't like to. There's her name, and there's what I call her.

KYLE

You were also gonna include her childhood sexual assault?

KATE

Yeah, I will add that, too, I just read you a part of it; I have a thing about that and, like other stuff. I'll add it, too. (*pause*) Yeah, yeah, there's more, plus, I'm not done. (*pause*) Maybe I am for now, though. (*pause*) Yeah, I'm done with this. I'm bored of it. For now.

>   *KATE shuts the laptop.*

KATE

I saved it. Just as a Word doc.

KYLE

Cool.

>   *Silence. KYLE offers himself to KATE. KATE moves near KYLE.*

KYLE

Do you wanna watch something? I saved the Egypt doc for us; I wanted to watch it so I can comment on the exhibit a bit better.

KATE

Yeah, no. Not really. I'm tired, but not in the mood for TV, just want –

KYLE
We could just...

KATE
... Yeah just, quiet –

KYLE
Sure.

> *KATE and KYLE settle into one another. A long moment of them just getting comfortable, in silence. KYLE starts to rub KATE's head. Then another long moment of being there, together, looking out, semi-comfortable.*
>
> *A loud knock.*

KYLE
Did you order weed or food or something?

KATE
No?

KYLE
I'll grab it.

KATE
Wait, should you? It's late.

KYLE
We live in Leslieville.

> *KYLE disappears. KATE is left on her own, visibly anxious. KYLE returns with RUBY.*

KYLE
You have a visitor.

RUBY
Hey.

KATE
Umm... Ruby? Hi? Uh, is everything okay? It's fucking late – and how do you kn–

RUBY
Dad told me.

KATE
He told you to come to my apartment, at, what time is it?

KYLE
Um, quarter to eleven.

RUBY
You didn't have to let me in, I asked at the door –

KYLE
Yeah that's, sorry, I invited her in, that's on me, I figured she's family.

RUBY
You blocked my number, so I couldn't give you a heads-up.

KYLE
(*to KATE*) Did you?

KATE
Did I? I can't remember.

    Beat.

RUBY
You did.

KATE

I believe you. (*pause*) You coulda done so through Dad, gave me a heads-up.

KYLE

Do you wanna drink, Ruby?

RUBY

Is that, do you mean– ?

KATE

Yeah.

RUBY

(*trying to be casual about alcohol, still getting used to the fact that she's legal*) Yeah, whatever you have… open, whatever.

KYLE disappears.

RUBY

Had to go back to Montréal for an exam before going back to The Soo to be with Mom. Took the Megabus, cheaper flying from Toronto.

KATE

Okay.

RUBY

Yeah. What?

KATE

Nothing.

Beat.

RUBY

Aren't you curious at all how she is?

KATE
I got an email from Woody.

RUBY
But I'm standing right in front of you.

KATE
You said you were in Montréal doing an exam. Woody's account is more recent anyway.

RUBY
I was with her for... months, I! Cared for her, the summer, and then moved her into hospice, I just had to be in Montréal – she wanted me to go. Fuck. It's been –

KYLE has returned with wine for RUBY.

KYLE
We're really sorry. Here.

KATE
Yeah, I'm sorry. It's been hard on you.

RUBY sips her wine, gives a slight nod, cold shoulder. A tense, long beat.

KATE
Okay, well, you've literally shown up at ours in the middle of the night.

RUBY
Do you want me to go?

KATE
No, just treat me with respect in my house while you drink my wine, please?

RUBY
What was disrespectful?

KATE
You know.

RUBY
Sorry you felt disrespected.

KYLE
So, do you need to crash here tonight, Ruby?

RUBY
No, I have a place I'm staying, thanks though.

KATE
You're welcome.

RUBY
Have a flight tomorrow. 9:30 a.m., so not too bad. It's cute in here. You've been here, what?

KATE
Over a year. Since I started my master's. (*pause*) You like McGill?

RUBY
Yeah, even though they've been a pain with Mom –

KATE
Your mom, ah, right –

RUBY
Our mom. They've been a pain with our mom dying, I was gonna say. (*pause*) Are you kidding me with this shit? You still won't call her your mom? I was going to see if you were maybe a more reasonable person than everyone in our

family thinks you are – and maybe you wanted a chance to come and see her, to redeem – I guess not.

KATE
"Everyone in our family."

RUBY
Me and Woody.

KATE
"Woody and I," you go to McGill for English.

RUBY
That just leaves Dad.

KATE
Yes, the only reasonable pers– the only adult in our family capable of keeping a job –

RUBY
I have a job. At the McGill library.

KYLE
I think she meant the only adult in that generation of your family who has kept a job.

RUBY
Um, Mom's organization for childhood sexual abuse healing, that's a job, duh.

KATE
I did mean that Kyle, thank you. And I meant a job, Ruby, not a website that she pays someone else to maintain with Woody's money. That's just Dad that's got one of those actual jobs, and as you well know, Dad's on my side.

KYLE
Hey – this isn't, come on.

RUBY
'Cause you have no one else, so he's afraid to see you for who you are, because you brainwashed him.

KATE
No, Ruby, I didn't, as a ten-year-old, brainwash him into thinking I was getting the shit kicked out of me by **OUR MOTHER**, I was just getting the shit kicked out of me by our mother.

RUBY
Where was I?

KATE
Being protected by the parent who you owe your life to. And me, for that matter. I protected you.

RUBY
That's some of your bullshit.

KATE
Leave. I didn't ask you to come here. If you think so little of me, stay away, that's what I'm doing. We don't need to have anything to do with one another 'cause we're family. That idea is horseshi– leave me alone. I'll leave you alone. You should go then, enjoy Sault Ste. Marie.

RUBY
You don't feel guilt at all?

KATE
My feelings are really not your business, Ruby. Since it's clear, like your mom, you don't have the maturity – I don't

have to justify, like – I am happy that she has you at the end. Actually.

RUBY
But she wants you.

KATE
I'm sure she does.

KYLE
You are?

KATE
I'm sure she is telling them she wants me, yes.

RUBY
She does. She asks for you all the time. She loves you.

KATE
Please stop.

RUBY
(*to* KYLE) You love her. Don't you want this for her?

KATE
Ruby, leave Kyle out of this.

KYLE
Why?

RUBY
Yeah, why?

KATE
Because you're my family, babe.

RUBY
Yeah, and so I'm his family, too –

KYLE
(*touched*) Aw, Ruby that's –

RUBY
Yeah, we're family –

KATE
I don't know what the point is of all this… language!

RUBY
You can't leave Kyle out of this!! Kyle is here!! Kyle is part of this!

KYLE
Thanks, Ruby, it's okay.

RUBY
No, don't thank me – I like you, I support you, Kyle.

KATE
Ruby, calm down, please.

RUBY
You have no idea how much Mom has wanted you, Kate, and how much she still does.

KATE
Holy shit. God. Ruby. This hurts.

RUBY
Yeah, it doesn't just hurt you.

KATE
I know, but it *also* hurts me.

RUBY
Well, we all know that's what really matters here.

KATE
Ruby, I know you've seen, like, her efforts with me at their beginning, but I've seen them through, Rubes, you understand? Any reasonableness I have, which, yes, may not be much, is 'cause I had to stay so with her, just to see if I was perfect, whether, y'know, she'd… I've offered her a fresh start, to never talk about the past, just the present and the future, which there is, ugh, so much of. So much to talk about. But she can't have any conversation with me that isn't disparaging Dad, she wants nothing else from me, and I've gone along with some of those – thought like, just let it get out of her system, then I can have a mom.

RUBY
You have a mom.

KATE
Stop. Listen to me – I've pretended to agree with stuff she's said about Dad, like, some stuff I do agree with, Dad is imperfect. But at the end of the day, he took care of me, she didn't, no one would have if he hadn't. Ruby, I have tried meeting all her conditions for her, fucking "unconditional love," and I've met them, too, but something eventually sets her off, okay, eventually: some tone in my voice, some perceived slight, and then she's the victim, of me and dad, and we're crazy, and she needs to protect herself and she's gone, like that, and it's my fault. I've walked this course so many times, Ruby. Every time, she finds a reason to just disappear.

RUBY
I've seen her crying after being on the phone with you. Oh, and she really is gonna disappear soon.

KATE

I've recorded our phone calls before, like, just to know that I'm not crazy, that I didn't say anything terrible. Even if I did, my future kid will say some shit to me and... I'll fight to know them and be there for... It's also not just that I want a mom, I want to be a daughter to her, too, Ruby, I have wanted that, but she can't admit that she really can't stand seeing me, so, so every fallout has always just – *must* be my fault, but it's not really, it's really just that she can't actually stand knowing me.

Beat.

KYLE

I guess what Ruby's saying, though, is that, well, all those concerns aren't really gonna matter, or they don't, like – she's on her deathbed, babe. She won't be able to talk shit about your dad.

RUBY

She won't even be able to talk to you, probably.

KYLE

I think Ruby's saying, like, your feelings are legitimate –

RUBY

I'm not.

KYLE

They're legitimate, I mean I'm saying they are, uh – but, are they, is this – worth hanging onto now, at this point?

KATE

Is what worth hanging onto? I had to let go of feelings for her, 'cause she kept... disappearing. Be like visiting a stranger –

RUBY
She's our mother –

KATE
I don't wish her any ill. I just don't know what it would mean at this point to visit, it wouldn't be sincere, would it?

RUBY
It would be for her comfort at the end of her life, and, like, you might want it, too, some redemption.

KATE
I don't think I have anything to be redeemed for. (*pause*) I don't wanna keep hurting myself to maintain some obligatory delusion, pretend I had something I didn't, and that it hurt me to not have.

KYLE
That's not what she's saying, you're not listening, babe.

KATE
I'm listening.

RUBY
No, he's right, you're not.

KATE
I am. (*pause*) Sorry, I think I am.

RUBY
Yeah, okay. (*pause*) As long as you're listening, then I'm saying you will regret this.

KATE
I hear you. I just disagree.

KYLE
Babe, I think you should consider what Ruby's saying.

KATE
Kyle, what the fuck are you doing?

RUBY
Stop!! He cares about you!

KATE
Is she here tonight 'cause, did you plan this, babe?

RUBY
Why do you attribute such evil motives to people who love y– him and, Mom –

KATE
I'm not attributing evil, I'm asking if you were in touch before, if he did this, and no one is telling me!

RUBY
'Cause you're being insane.

KATE
Ruby? What motives would you attribute to this? So, do you remember this one time, Mom was driving, you were five, I was ten. I was in the front seat and Mom was just, like, punching me in the face, again and again as she drove, and she was yelling, because she'd been yelling and you got scared and wouldn't stop crying, and I said if she stopped yelling you might stop? So she was just driving at, like, eighty, left hand on the wheel, right hand just punching me in the face, my jaw, oh my God it burrrrned, my mouth was bleeding all over this blue shirt I had and loved with a monkey on it riding a bike, it was from Reitmans. I lost a tooth, and this guy driving on the road next to us in a black Honda, he saw her from his car and chased us for,

like, I don't know, maybe five minutes, not long, but he
had his window down and was yelling at her that she was
a bitch and how dare she hit her kid like that, and she was,
like, yelling at me that it was all my fault and he was crazy
and would probably kill her and it would be my fault, and
you were crying and then she was, like, in a nice voice, like,
"Aww, Ruby, don't cry," then screaming at me and punching
me more and, like, pointing at my tooth in my hand saying
look what I'd done, it was all my fault, and then when she
lost the guy chasing her, like, when he turned down another
road eventually, she pulled over and made me get out of the
car and left me there on the side of the road, I was ten, and,
like, I walked, it was the county, I walked maybe fifteen or
twenty minutes to a Becker's – remember Becker's? – and,
like, used the phone, and Dad came and got me, we got a
freezie for my jaw, do you remember that?

RUBY
No.

KATE
You were little.

KYLE
Babe.

RUBY
I do remember there always being something, some reason
for you to fucking freak out. All the time. I remember Mom
getting overwhelmed by it, yeah, and trying to give me some,
some attention and time and like, love, because Dad was
always all about you, it all revolved around you.

KATE
Dad saw what she did to me, so yeah, he compensated
and coddled – for sure. I've had to draw boundaries, it's a
different relationship, but he loves you so much, Ruby.

RUBY
I know. Fuck off.

KATE
He misses you.

RUBY
Fuck yourself, Dad and I talk, you don't know our relationship. (*pause*) I remember you getting nosebleeds a lot.

KATE
A nosebleed is when your nose randomly starts bleeding for no reason. You remember my nose bleeding because I got hit in the face all the time. (*pause*) Also, Dad: you've had a relationship because he's given you a choice, he wouldn't ever make it so all or nothing.

RUBY
(*to KYLE*) How do you not just find her unbearable most of the time? (*to KATE*) How serious could you and Dad have taken your own abuse and, like, the threat of Mom, if you left me with her when I was seven?

KATE
You don't know how hard Dad tried to get you and keep you safe, Rubes. I was old enough to say I wanted to live with him. Proving stuff against a mother is hard.

RUBY
That's bullshit, no one has any problem judging women and mothers as terrible people. You should know, as you actually are a terrible person, and everyone comes to that conclusion pretty quickly with you.

KATE

Do you realize, Ruby, that I've not called you horrible things in this conversation, and that you have to me, like, with everything you've said to me? Are you able to see that, or have you bought into this myth, this brainwashing from her, that I'm such a piece of shit you can say whatever to me and treat me however and it doesn't count? I'm not perfect, no, been trying to climb out of this, like, hole she put me in, forever. I'm getting, you know, there, but fuck, you show up and say – Do you see why I don't wanna go see her?

RUBY

No. No, I don't.

KATE

I know what you're saying is coming from her, so it doesn't help the case when you say horrible things to me. I'm not perfect, but I have no hope if I spend all my time hearing this.

RUBY

Actually, I think you need to hear this.

KATE

What?

RUBY

This!

KATE

What? – Say it.

RUBY

I did – that you're an asshole. (*pause*) Do you have a therapist?

KATE
Not right at this point. So expensive. I belong to, like, I don't know, therapy-type groups.

RUBY
Pardon?

KYLE
Like, support groups.

RUBY
Do you support that?

KYLE
Of course.

RUBY
You're part of the group?

KYLE
What? No.

RUBY
Just supportive of the support –

KYLE
A supporter of the support gr– ha, yes…

Beat.

RUBY
What types of groups? (*pause*) How do they advertise themselves?

Silence.

Well? Support with what? (*pause*) Hmm? Support with being a piece of shit?

KATE
Yes, Ruby.

KYLE
No, they're online groups, motherless daughter, that kind of stuff.

RUBY
Oh my God.

KATE
Kyle! Come on –

KYLE
What?

RUBY
Sooooo sad.

KATE
Why?

RUBY
Just like, cults can exist online now, of course, you don't have to be in one physical place.

KYLE
They aren't cults.

KATE
They're support groups. Would you prefer I did nothing?

RUBY

You basically are doing nothing. (*pause*) She sent you Christmas cards every year.

KATE

While not so much as an email on my birthday or any other time.

RUBY

You can't expect people to stay if you treat them like shit. Not even your own mother. (*to KYLE*) Are you figuring her out? (*to KATE*) He's figuring you out. He'll probably fucking run away in the night.

KYLE

I'm not. I know what I'm in for.

KATE

Oh yeah?

KYLE

What you're like sometimes, yeah.

KATE

And what's that, then?

KYLE

I don't know, like, here we are, talking about what you're like.

RUBY

Exactly.

> *Beat.*

KATE

Kyle. (*pause*) Okay. (*pause*) (*to RUBY*) Okay, you know what? Stop – I was talking about how Dad loves you, *you* brought it around to the fact that I'm unbearable. (*pause*) Dad loves you.

RUBY
You are being manipulative and you know it, I've never, ever called into question his love for me. You're trying to make me.

KATE
I'm not trying to do anything!

RUBY
Mom never cut you off. She just insisted you not be terrible to her, and you could never do that. While she was healing herself from actual sexual abuse that she, like, had as a child, Kate. She's done good things for people who suffered like she did. And you were horrible to her. And Dad puts up with it, so you have this messed-up expectation of what people are supposed to put up with from you.

KATE
I was a needy kid, and I'm sometimes a needy adult. I'm working on myself.

RUBY
You can't just say that. That doesn't fix anything, and it's just not fair.

KATE
To who?

RUBY
Just... not fair, generally.

KATE
That doesn't make sense.

RUBY
Yes, it does, there is fair and unfair, you fucking idiot.

KATE
Ruby. That's mean. I love you.

RUBY
You say it to make me feel guilty and, like, you're better than me, so it doesn't count, actually.

KATE
I guess I should just never say it then.

    Beat.

RUBY
Yeah, please. Don't say it to me.

    Silence.

Mom had this quote framed in her room for years, next to a photo of you when you're a baby and one from your middle-school graduation –

KATE
Oh yeah, which she wasn't at –

RUBY
Still has it, in the house though, not with her at the hospice, we left it there – but this quote that's framed, it's "The better you feel, the better chance you have of a life without her, and actually the better chance you have of a life with her."

KATE
I'm glad she could use me as a reason for her to feel better. That's what parenting is all about. I'm sure she probably thinks she's a victim of parental alienation or some shit.

RUBY
Well, yeah.

KATE
And who is meant to have done the alienating? Dad?

RUBY
That's what she thinks.

KATE
And you think that's plausible?

RUBY
No, I think she's blaming Dad because she can't bring herself to blame you.

KATE
Oh, right.

RUBY
I think you brainwashed Dad, and he knows that to keep you from fucking killing yourself he has to take your side.

KATE
(*to* KYLE) Can you get her out? (*to* RUBY) You're fucked, girl.

KYLE
(*to* KATE) Hey – no, you don't wan–

KATE
No, no! Don't fucking say "hey" to me, Kyle, you let her into our place – at the end of what was a really hard night for me, and then she began verbally attacking me –

RUBY
Oh, there we go, y'victim!

KATE
You're in my house! Get out if you find me so unreasonable and off-putting, I didn't ask you to come over at 11 p.m. on a weekday – I don't profess to be able to avoid stepping in the traps you fucking set for me –

RUBY
You're a fucking lunatic, we walk on eggshells to make you comfortable **AND MOM IS DYING, DO YOU UNDERSTAND**, and Mom feels **GUILTY!!!** That's what kills me!!

KATE
You don't know what you're talking **ABOUT! JUST GET THE FUCK OUT!!**

KYLE
HEY! –

KATE
DON'T MANAGE ME, I'm not! – You can actually be the most gentle, dominating person!!!

RUBY
YOU DON'T DESERVE HIM OR ANYTHING OR ANYONE –

KATE
GET OUT!!

RUBY
HE'S TRYING AND MOM – MOM HAS TRIED AND TRIED AND IS DYING TRYING AND TRYING AND –

KATE
YOU DON'T KNOW WHAT YOU'RE TALKING ABOUT WITH HER – RUBY – THERE IS A DIFFERENCE

BETWEEN GUILT AND SELF-PITYING – OKAY? DID YOU KNOW THAT? GET OUT.

RUBY
(*to* KYLE) I'm so sorry for you.

>   KATE *attacks* RUBY. KYLE *pulls* KATE *off* RUBY.

KATE
I never wanted you here!! You walked into my house and deliberately, to, just so you could have something to report to her – FUCK YOU, YOU DELUDED, COWARDLY...

KYLE
STOP!!!!

KATE
Did you see her? How fucking dare she?

RUBY
I'm leaving.

KYLE
You're bleeding, she's – ? What? Okay no, no, can we just cool off and, like, take a moment, to, um, repair her, and you, and things, before she goes. She will go.

KATE
Fine.

RUBY
I'm fine.

KYLE
No, no – let me see? (*like a conflict-averse* TV *dad, trying to normalize*) Ah. (*pause*) Sisters. (*pause*) One second.

KYLE disappears. KATE and RUBY sit in silence. RUBY has the power. KATE is ashamed.

RUBY
How do you think you would deal with you, as a parent? Can you admit you were a difficult kid?

KATE
Kyle!!! Can you come back here, please?

RUBY
Need a guy to hide behind, sounds right.

KYLE comes back.

KYLE
I'm back! I brought rubbing alcohol, which might be a bit much.

KATE
Pour it in her fucking eyes –

KYLE
Rubbing alcohol might be too much, but there's Polysporin and here, Band-Aids, take your pick of sizes.

RUBY
What luxury treatment.

KATE
I'm sorry, Ruby. You crossed a line. I shoulda watched while you crossed it and not retaliated.

RUBY
That's kind of an apology, I guess. I don't think I crossed any physical lines.

KATE
I didn't say you did.

KYLE
You goaded her, though.

RUBY
Excuse me? Aren't you an adult that's responsible for your abusive, aggressive behaviour, regardless of whether someone is getting under your skin? Isn't that –

KYLE
Okay, I'd go with that size of Band-Aid. Don't worry, we have a few, so you won't be putting us out if you use it. (*pause*) It's been a big day for her. We had a long night.

RUBY
Were you fighting?

KATE
No. I was writing an honest obituary for her. That I might post on Facebook, since I doubt I'll have any say in the one you write for the organization's website –

RUBY
What the fuck? Pardon?

KATE
Yeah –

KYLE
Hey –

KATE
Yeah, so I'll post my obituary for her on Facebook when she dies. You deleted me off there, but I can email it to you if you want?

RUBY
You better fucking not.

KATE
Oh yeah?

RUBY
Everyone who reads it – and I mean **EVERYONE** – will take her side. Mom is a hero to so many fucking people, Kate, and rightfully so, she's earned that, because she came back from actual abuse and helped others. Everyone will take her side. It's not even a – everyone. People who don't even know her. Even your stupid friends will see right through you, everyone sees right through you.

KATE
(*to* KYLE) I'm gonna kill her if we don't kick her out.

KYLE
This feels like a terrible note to end things on, though.

RUBY
We are completely done if you post that shit.

KATE
As if we weren't now alr–

KYLE
She isn't going to – she just, she wrote it for herself, as an excer–

RUBY
I'm sure she did do it for herself; it and everything else she does.

KATE
Do you wanna read it?

KYLE
What the fuck is happening?! Let her go.

KATE
She's still here, despite my having asked her to go, despite her not having been invited in the first – so maybe she wants to read what I'm gonna post about our mother as soon as she croaks.

RUBY
I will be sure to personally write to all of your Facebook friends, and the people at U of T in your department, **EVERYONE**, and make sure they know what kind of a person you are if you –

KATE
And what kind of a perso–

KYLE
STOP!!! Fucking stop it, now!! I've had enough!! I'm done.

RUBY
Oh, man of the house calling the shots. Wait, done with her?

KYLE
I don't – no.

KATE
What?

KYLE
No, I'm not done with you.

KATE
Oh my God, babe.

KYLE
Sorry.

KATE
Don't apologize, just this is why I don't let this toxic family shit in.

KYLE
You attacked her!

KATE
I know! I'm sorry.

KYLE
I've never seen that before fr–

KATE
I've never done that before!

RUBY
Liar.

KATE
As an adult, Ruby. I fought back Mom, as a kid, yeah, until I stopped living with her so, eleven. That's not old, Ruby. Bit different, no? And I never hit you when we were kids, did I?

RUBY
I don't remember.

KATE
I didn't, you don't remember because I fucking didn't, ugh! I'm so fucking done being dragged back into this fantasy world, you have Stockholm syndrome from Mom and you, you exploit Kyle's good will, to come into my house –

RUBY
Who do you feel exploited by right now, Kyle?

KATE
RUBY, ENOUGH. GO!

> *KATE pushes RUBY across the floor. RUBY drops her phone. KATE backs off.*

RUBY
Oh, fuck.

KYLE
(*picking up the phone and giving it to RUBY*) It didn't crack, it's fine.

RUBY
No. (*pause, looking at her phone*) I – no. Oh my God. (*pause*) Oh my God.

> *Long beat.*

I don't wanna be here right now.

KATE
Well, we've been trying to get you to go for –

KYLE
What is it? She's upset. Are you hurt, Ruby?

KATE
I can see she's upset. She's not hurt. (*pause*) Ruby?

> *Beat. RUBY is frozen.*

RUBY
No. No, I don't want to talk to…

>*Long beat.*

KATE
Then go.

KYLE
No. We're not kicking you out, Ruby.

KATE
We are.

KYLE
No. We aren't.

>*Beat.*

KATE
Okay.

RUBY
Shut up. Fuck. (*pause*) You.

>*Long silence. There is clearly something on RUBY's phone that has silenced her. She can't look at KYLE or KATE. RUBY seems angry, like she could cry, but she doesn't.*

>*KATE pees herself. No one notices, except KATE, who goes and sits and covers herself with the blanket. She uses the edge of the blanket with her foot to get some of the trail she left. KYLE notices, but doesn't pursue it, noticing KATE's attempted discreetness and her humiliation.*

KYLE
Ruby?

RUBY
I don't...

Long beat. Everyone knows what's coming.

I. I got a, a text. I don't, from Woody? We agreed on a code word – ? This text is from six minutes ago, that's what I don't get, that's what – why did I just see – six minutes? (*pause*) How did I – like... Yeah. (*pause*) We had a code word, 'cause we all know it's going to happen, right, no one wanted to feel bad for not being there and have to get some call, the moment is insignificant, it's all the other moments that count.

Beat.

KYLE
Did she... die?

Beat.

RUBY
"Bubble" was the code word. I just got a, well not just, like seven minutes ago, from Woody. "Bubble." He put a period at the end, fucking creep.

Beat.

KYLE
Oh. (*pause*) We don't like him either!

RUBY
Kyle, you've never met him. (*pause*) Kate only met him, like, twice.

Beat.

I didn't say I didn't like him, anyway.

> *Silence.* KATE *is sitting in her own urine. It begins to be obvious she has peed herself.*

KYLE
Babe. Are you?

RUBY
What happened?

> *Beat.*

Hmm – ?

> *Beat.*

Oh. (*pause*) Ew.

> KATE *disappears and changes clothes.* RUBY *and* KYLE *stand in silence.*

KYLE
I'm sorry.

> KYLE *tries to think of something more to say.* RUBY *wants him to say something, too.* KATE *returns.*

KATE
Okay. (*pause*) Ruby. Ruby, what can I do for you?

> *Beat.*

Ruby. I'm sorry. (*pause*) I'm so sorry, Ruby. Can I hug you?

RUBY
No.

KATE
Can Kyle?

RUBY
No.

KYLE
Well, I'm not doing anything without your consent!

KATE
No one said otherwi–

KYLE
Yeah, sor–

KATE
Your dad, I kno–

RUBY
What about his dad?

KATE
He's a creep.

RUBY
Oh.

KATE
Kyle's afraid of becoming that.

RUBY
Ah.

Beat. KYLE *nods to himself.*

RUBY
: (*to* KYLE) Mom liked you.

KATE
: She never met him, Ruby.

RUBY
: Doesn't matter. (*to* KYLE) Anyone who can make that one happy. (*pause*) Does she call all the shots when you fuck?

KATE
: Ruby!

RUBY
: My mom just died!!

KATE
: I know!!

RUBY
: Our mom!

KATE
: Yup.

RUBY
: What? Well!! Is she or not?! Do you even care she's dead?! Agh! You're a horrible person. Probably peed yourself with excitement and fucking, joy!

> Beat. KATE *ever so privately and quietly considers that this might be true.*

KATE
: Do you, do you wanna stay here tonight? (*pause*) You should: we could set you up on the couch. Kyle drives, eh, if you have stuff you need to collect from anywhere.

KYLE
    Do you have stuff that you need to collect from anywhere, Ruby? We can grab that tonight, if you need.

RUBY
    I don't have stuff. (*pause, then to* KYLE) You could drive me to the airport for, like, 8:30 tomorrow?

KATE
    You don't need to get there that early, it's non-international.

KYLE
    I work though, so earlier is better for me.

RUBY
    Oh, no, if you work – no. I'll Uber. Sorry.

KYLE
    No, I can –

RUBY
    No, no –

KYLE
    Okay, that's easier for me if you Uber.

KATE
    But he can also drive you.

RUBY
    I'll Uber.

    Silence.

RUBY
    (*to* KATE) Can you not look at me, please?

>   *Beat.*

KATE
   Sure.

>   *Beat.*

Sure.

>   *Beat.*

(*not looking at her*) You know. (*pause*) I love you so much, Ruby.

RUBY
   Can you not?

KATE
   And her. So when, like, I used to babysit in high school, I used to imagine when I was holding those kids that I was holding her, and you know, I have dreams about it, actually sometimes still, like she's a child, like five or six, I don't even know how I know it's her, I just do and I'm, you know, cuddling her, taking care, whatever, of her.

>   *Beat.*

RUBY
   Is that supposed to, like, make me think you're a fucking good person or something? That's what you could have done in the hospice and you didn't. Don't look at me!! I said I don't wanna see your stupid fa–

KATE
   You don't know what I –? With Mom it's always only been able to be fantasies for me, Ruby, so I know it maybe seems… but you don't know what's in my mind, Rubes, what

fantasies I've entertai– fuck, I've had to get by on just this, so this is no different this time right, so.

RUBY
You called her Mom just now, by the way.

KATE
I know. I did it for your sake.

RUBY
You looked exactly like her just now. Toronto has UberPool, right?

KATE
Um, yeah. (*pause*) Right, Kyle? I think so.

KYLE
Yeah.

RUBY
How far is the airport?

KYLE
Is it Porter?

RUBY
Yeah.

KATE
Then it's not far at all.

RUBY
'Kay. Great.

Long beat.

Kyle, can you hug me?

KYLE
Sure.

> *KYLE hugs RUBY. KATE watches.*
>
> *Beat.*
>
> *KYLE returns to his seat.*

KATE
I'll get the couch set up.

KYLE
Do you need help?

KATE
No, stay with her.

> *KATE disappears.*

RUBY
I should maybe call Woody. I don't feel like it right now, though.

KYLE
You don't have to do anything you don't feel like.

RUBY
That's sweet, ha – thanks –

KYLE
Ever!

RUBY
Well, that's not true.

KYLE
Ha, true ... Ah.

Beat.

RUBY
Does your dad know he's a creep?

KYLE
No.

RUBY
Oh.

KYLE
Yeah.

RUBY
You should let him know at some point.

KYLE goes to speak, then sees that KATE is walking in – and thinks twice. He nods at RUBY semi-appreciatively (but he will never bring it up with his dad and doesn't want KATE to get that idea in her head). KATE returns with bedding and starts to set up the couch nicely with sheets, duvet, and pillow.

KATE
Do you want a glass of water?

RUBY
I'm a grown-up, I have a reusable water bottle in my bag.

KATE
Great.

KYLE gets up and starts fussing around, turning off lights.

RUBY
Are you just... going to... go to bed? (*pause*) Kate, do you think Mom, or whatever the fuck you call her –

KATE
Yes –

RUBY
No. I don't know what I was going to – maybe I just don't want you to go to bed. This is – I mean, I have my own apartment in Montréal, sometimes I buy wine and don't drink it right away, it just sits in my kitchen, unopened, I'm *definitely* an adult... but more so, like... right now.

KATE
Are you drinking a lot?

RUBY
Wait, I just realized Mom is dead and I haven't cried, is that, what is that, do you think?

KYLE
Shock. I was the same way when my uncle Paul died.

KATE
I want to go to bed, Ruby. I have feelings about this too that I don't wanna have in front of someone who will attack me for them.

RUBY
Why would I attack you?

KATE
Ruby, if I say that I buried Mom years ago?

Beat.

(*to* KYLE) Can you give us …? I don't need … it's – yeah.

KYLE
Yup, cool! Great.

KYLE *disappears.*

RUBY
How did you meet him, by the way?

KATE
What? Oh. University, beginning of – we were friends awhile first.

RUBY
University: how, though, like actually?

KATE
I don't know, I went up to him and started talking to him like I knew him, and then I did.

RUBY
Okay. I'm not gonna attack you. For whatever you wanna say about Mom. It just makes me sad for you. You missed out.

KATE
No Ruby – that's not – no. You don't know what you're talking about: it used to send my body into a panic to be around her. You can't make yourself a better person for the people who need you if you're subjecting yourself to bodily terror every few months. And when I'm afraid, I'm not my best version of myself, that's, I mean, I sometimes took the high road with her and sometimes didn't.

RUBY
Yeah. You missed out.

Beat.

You didn't get to see how she, like, grew, like, in the last, I don't know, year? She did a lot of good through her organization, for the kids or whatever. Yeah, but like, yeah, then when she got really, really sick, she just really, yeah, got softer she... grew. (*pause*) I'm just actually, like, so proud of her. (*pause*) I hope, like, I think. I think she knew.

KATE
Oh I'm sure, Ruby. She totally, yeah, would've.

Beat.

RUBY
She was hilarious and vibrant and cool and weird and free. She didn't shave her armpits before it was cool. (*pause*) She didn't put up with anyone's shit, including yours.

KATE
I was a kid.

RUBY
You were psychotic.

KATE
She told me that every day till I felt it, at least.

RUBY
People aren't perfect, Kate, but she tried so hard to be for you, right till the end. She had a temper, she could also be a really good mom.

KATE
No, Ruby, *no. Fuck. I* have a temper –

RUBY
You're damn right you do. You attacked me! How is that different than her?

KATE
Yes, I'm sorry. It was bad of me. I am so, so sorry. I'm – it was – I love you, I wanna be here for you –

RUBY
Answer my ques– how is it any different?

KATE
Because of the power differential, Ruby, you're my peer, she's my mother –

RUBY
I'm your *little* sister! I'm five years younger!

KATE
No, Ruby, you're an adult! You just said so – you're not a child!!

> *RUBY starts to cry.* KATE *approaches her and tentatively puts a hand on* RUBY's *shoulder.* RUBY *likes this and tries to receive it openly and stay in it, but is also self-conscious about being seen as asking for affection from this person she has complicated feelings toward.*

RUBY
I want to see whatever thing you wrote about her.

KATE
Oh oh, no, it's not... I don't know that you'd like it. Or that now is the time.

RUBY
Now is definitely the time.

KATE
It's private.

RUBY
Show me. You threatened to, didn't you? You were like, "the obituary I'll post *when she croaks*," REMEMBER?!

KATE
Fuck, RUBY, I'm so sorry! GOD, I'M SO SORRY. I'm awful – FUCK!!

KYLE re-enters.

KYLE
Is everything...?

KATE
YES!! I'm sorry to yell!

KYLE
No, I'm sorry to hover!

KATE
It's fine babe!

KYLE
'Kay, gonna disappear again – !

KATE
'Kay – wait!

RUBY
No – *SHOW* ME –

KYLE
Show what?

KATE
No, no –

RUBY
The obituary Kate wr–

KYLE
No.

KATE
I already said no, it's my no.

RUBY
It's not your no. My mom just died. (*pause*) Don't say yours did, too.

KATE
I wasn't going to.

RUBY
What were you gonna say, then?

KATE
Nothing.

RUBY
What?

KATE
Nothing.

RUBY
What, what were you thinking?

KATE
Um, I was thinking 'bout how, I don't know, like, a healthy long-term relationship means looking in the eyes of someone who knows your shit and seeing what they think of you at any moment and not looking away and I do that, Ruby, with Kyle – you were asking about our relationship before.

RUBY
I asked how you met. Stop trying to change the topic to something you can be fucking superior about. I wanna see the obituary.

KATE
Do you think Mom saw my shit? 'Cause I think, I think she thought I could see hers better than she saw mine, and she couldn't have that, she couldn't stand going back to people who knew her deal, right, but I can do that.

RUBY
You're saying I didn't know Mom really and you did and really, really, you don't know fucking anything. You're not fucking forty years old, shut up. (*pause*) You need to show me the thing.

KATE
No.

RUBY
Like you could even see past yourself, she was sensitive and vulnerable and you never fucking –

KATE
I WAS THE CHILD!!! –

RUBY
SHOW ME THE OBIT –

KATE
Fine!

KYLE
Hey!

KATE
Fuck! Fine.

KYLE
No. Babe.

KATE
It's fine.

KYLE
Absolutely not.

> *KATE punches her password into her laptop and picks it up.*

KYLE
Hey... What?... (*pause*) Hey...

KATE
(*approaching* RUBY *with her laptop*) I was gonna add how she and Granny were... raped, as kids. I thought that would be nice, I wouldn't put it like that – but like, "childhood sexual abuse victim," "systems failed them" – I tried to make it a lot about systems.

RUBY
Nice. (*pause*) Give it.

KYLE
No – stop. No. I'm sorry, I'm not letting this happen, you're both in shock and can't make this call for yourselves right now, so I'm stepping in.

RUBY
Pardon?

> RUBY *snatches the laptop off* KATE, *who doesn't resist, and starts reading.*

KYLE
Ruby!

KATE
You're being fucking strange and paternalistic. Why don't you step in with your own family, where you have something to lose, huh? This is not your life.

KYLE
Excuse me?

KATE
Back off, our mom just died. (*pause*) What? Go to bed?

> KATE *makes the order clear.* KYLE *doesn't move. Then he goes and sits, shaking his head. Once he does,* KATE *feels she's won.* RUBY *reads a while in silence as* KATE *watches her.*

RUBY
Woah.

KATE
What? What part are you on?

RUBY
No, just ... all of it.

KATE
But what part are you on?

RUBY
"1999 sobriety period."

KATE
Her travelling!

RUBY
Travelling. India.

KATE
Nice. Keep reading.

RUBY keeps reading.

KYLE
I'm going to bed.

KATE
You pissed?

KYLE
Yeah, I'm fucking pissed.

KATE
Is it 'cause I pissed?

KYLE
It's not 'cause you – fucking stop.

KATE
You want me to stop taking the piss?

RUBY
Can you shut up! My kind of ADHD makes it impossible to read if you talk!

KYLE
That's fine. I don't need to talk to Kate at all anymore, actually.

KATE
Babe?

KYLE
I'm going to bed, remember, I have nothing to lose here.

KYLE is gone.

KATE
What, did I say he had nothing to lose here, or something?

RUBY
Yeah, like, just now.

KATE
Oh. I didn't get that. He's bad at being angry. I think he thinks it's an admirable quality in him. So do I.

RUBY
Shut up, I'm barely halfway.

RUBY reads a little longer in silence.

KATE
Do you think he's actually mad?

RUBY
Yeah.

KATE
  Really?

RUBY
  Shhh, reading...

KATE
  ... I can fix...

RUBY
  Shh...

  RUBY reads on.

  A shift. RUBY *has gotten to the spot. They both know it.* RUBY *reads on. Then she stops.*

RUBY
  Oh, I don't think I was abused, you have to take that out. Just say one of her children, if you really have to. But no, actually no, no, just take that out.

KATE
  Rubes.

RUBY
  Also – where was? – can you take out where you call her "frighteningly delusional"? And add something about how loved she was in spite of all the bad stuff we say? And I wanna add some details about the organization and it's core mission and about, like, how she lived and was at the end – like, yeah, she and I *did* have that couple years of estrangement, so that's fact, you can print that, I guess –

KATE
  What? You craz– like, what? Rubes, facts? What, what about the fact of her hurting you?

RUBY
She didn't.

KATE
She did.

RUBY
She went back and got her master's, like, three years ago, remember? Adding that.

KATE
What? No! Give me my laptop, Ruby.

RUBY
No. Did Dad buy it for you?

KATE
Give it back!!

RUBY
No!

>   *RUBY moves to avoid KATE, who doesn't have the energy to pursue her. RUBY keeps her attention on the laptop.*

RUBY
No. I'll add a paragraph, just, like, some of my things I wanna say about how she, like, was, and led the family and stuff. I'll take out – yeah, 'cause I think with my edits, like, it's nice in parts, we can use a lot of what you – the system stuff is, is nice, and I do just wanna talk about her. Like. Her life, all of it, in a *real* way, you know? Fuck. This just feels so fucking weird. I just don't wanna ever stop talking about her.

>   *Beat.*

KATE
Ruby, we're not going to post anything.

RUBY
Why not?

KATE
I don't know.

RUBY
Why not? You have to answer – because I want to now?

KATE
No.

RUBY
Because you actually wanted Mom to see this while she was still alive.

KATE
No. No, Ruby there's no way you actually want to post it. You're just trying to distract yourself by doing something. Give me that.

RUBY
No.

KATE
Just let me look at it.

RUBY
Fine.

Side by side, KATE *and* RUBY *check out the laptop. They read in silence.*

KATE
I can't – you really, like?

RUBY
Yeah. I mean. Yeah, so the part about periods of substance abuse, addiction, violent rages, yeah so, keep "substance abuse and addiction" stuff, take out abuse… abuse. You know? Yeah?

KATE
Are you?

RUBY
That shouldn't be the only thing we say, but it won't be, like, you don't have this perspective on Mom that's, like, so unique, you just handled it differently. I think even the people, like, who didn't know her as well would, like, not be – it might probably explain a lot of, like, her limits with them that maybe they were taking personally.

KATE
You think all that is true, but you don't think that you or I were abused?

RUBY
No, I think *she* was abused. And sometimes an addict, probably always an addict. Had personality-disorder stuff, challenges she was ashamed of, didn't wanna be confronted 'bout and didn't, like, overcome fully, and I don't mind, like, mentioning that. Or sharing it, whatever. She also did a lot of just amazing things. And I think we should write something, like as, you know, her two kids, together, that reflects all that.

Beat.

KATE
Rube.

RUBY
Why not? We won't post *this*, yes, of course, we'll work on something together. I just, just wanna talk about her with people.

KATE
On Facebook? Now?

RUBY
Tonight or tomorrow morning we should. Before I go.

KATE
No.

RUBY
Why not? We'll agree on what we p–

KATE
No.

RUBY
Why not? 'Cause you're scared we won't agree?

KATE
No.

RUBY
What?

KATE
Um, I don't actually think you're going to ... feel the same way about this over the next, like, while, for one. And 'cause how we feel doesn't, um, matter as much as, I don't know, the idea of her life.

RUBY
What?

KATE
The idea of her life, um, I don't know, like...?

RUBY
No – no, you're just pulling that out of your ass, like, as an excuse: the idea of her life as an excuse to not talk to me about her life. No, you, somehow you wrote something pretty articulate and kinda nice –

KATE
Don't need y–

RUBY
Yeah, in places, and a lot, like, about the systems failing her, which they so fucking did. So just let me, I'll just take out the –

KATE
No, no, then it's not! –

RUBY
Yeah, a few bits, let me take out, yeah, like, obviously the physical abuse –

KATE
What? But that's the *whole point*?!

RUBY
No the whole point is she grew up in a harder world than we did! And she managed! Imperfectly, like, just like everyone, fucking, she managed!! God! God. God, I feel *so different*. We had a code word, we had "bubble" 'cause it wasn't supposed to feel sudden, it's not sudden, she's been so bad for so long. We knew, right, but it – feels fast, like, who

am I accountable to, who are we accountable to now but to ourselves? Doesn't it feel...?

> KATE *takes the laptop from* RUBY. *She puts in on the table.* RUBY *is more giddy than sad.*

RUBY
Did you just have a feeling tonight?

KATE
What do you mean?

RUBY
When did you write this thing?

KATE
Tonight. (*pause*) Look we should forget about this okay, it –

RUBY
No, I'll add something about the ways she grew at the end of her life, take out the physical abuse stuff, and some other stuff, we'll work it together, but I do want to post it. I had a feeling tonight, I think I had a feeling.

KATE
No.

RUBY
What?

KATE
Ruby come on, this doesn't reflect, you know this, who she wanted to be, who she was with a lot of other people, what she maintained, we gotta give her that.

RUBY
She was scared people wouldn't accept certain parts of her, but they would, even *posthumously* – boom-McGill-English-what?

KATE
No, the org– the whole community there –

RUBY
We're not allowed to have our thing be true, because it might shit on their thing they think is true?

KATE
It can be true without it going on Facebook.

RUBY
Not really.

Beat.

No, no, look: I'm saying we'd write one, that isn't this. But would look something like, like, it. Like, it could, like, discuss some of her challenges, and how she struggled with them, things she felt ashamed of, but wasn't in control of, was victim, like, to… We can't make her, she didn't, she didn't abuse anyone except verbally a bit maybe, so editing that and –

KATE
NO! NO, it's mine, you're not – we're not – and she *did*, she did, she abused you, she hurt you, *physically*, I saw it, *fuck*.

RUBY
Yeah, she could be rough. She totally could be: she was tough, she didn't back down or apologize, she was strong, **NOT** abusive – / you can't put that.

KATE

There is no Facebook obit from me then, that's what I have to say, all those things or / nothing at all.

RUBY

She didn't put up with your shit, and you'd be a better person if you'd been raised by her and not Dad, who let you get away with / everything.

KATE

Wait, Ruby – "She could be rough," you just, what do you – what?

RUBY

Don't post something horrible about her by yourself after I get on the plane tomorrow.

Beat.

Please, Kate.

KATE

I knew it, that's the... that's the reason you wanna write something together.

RUBY

There are a lot of people who love her.

KATE

Just to shut me up. I just d– wait – Ruby: "She could be rough"? Ruby, you just – yeah? You said it, just now? Right?

RUBY

Yeah, for sure she could be. (*pause*) You had it worst for sure, 'cause you're you and you're alike. (*pause*) You're both so...

Beat.

KATE
Yes?

RUBY
Angry.

> *As long a beat as* KATE *feels like taking.*

KATE
I have to go to bed.

> *Beat.*

RUBY
Really?

KATE
Yeah.

> *Beat.*

RUBY
Why?

> *Beat.*

KATE
I could sleep here?

RUBY
No.

> *Beat.*

KATE
'Kay. (*pause*) You want me to turn this?

RUBY
Course, I sleep in the dark.

Beat.

KATE
Okay. Cool.

RUBY
Yup.

KATE
Sweet.

RUBY
Yeah.

Beat. KATE starts to leave.

KATE
Goodnight.

Beat. KATE seems to linger, waits a moment for RUBY to stop her. RUBY doesn't.

RUBY
Night, sister.

KATE
Night. (*pause*) Whatever you need tomorrow, eh.

RUBY
I'm gonna set my alarm and Uber to the airport.

KATE
Oh. Right. Have you talked to Woody?

RUBY
We texted.

KATE
Okay.

>   *Beat.*

What?

RUBY
No, just feel kinda bad for him. Wonder what he'll do now.

KATE
Yeah.

>   *Beat.*

Well. (*pause*) Goodnight. (*pause*) You want the light out, yeah?

RUBY
Yup, as I already said.

KATE
Did you?

RUBY
I'm willing to post all what you wrote, just not that one thing.

KATE
Willing to or want to?

RUBY
Both.

KATE
 Big difference.

RUBY
 You're getting most of what you want, just not all of what you want.

KATE
 I don't want any of it I don't wanna post.

RUBY
 How did it just change?

KATE
 It just... did.

RUBY
 You just don't wanna think about her anymore.

   Beat.

 I'm willing to agree with all of your whole account except one thing – you need to have your way or nothing, though, like: 'cause I won't call our mom, who was an actual abuse survivor, who fought hard to come back from it and then helped actual survivors, 'cause I won't call her an abuser, you just can't even talk to me about her.

   Beat.

KATE
 We can talk about this more another time, maybe.

   Beat.

RUBY
 When?

> *Beat.*

KATE
  I have to go to bed. (*pause*) Okay? (*pause*) Okay. (*pause*) Okay. (*pause*) Goodnight.

> *Beat.*

I told you I'd sleep here if you wanted.

RUBY
  No.

KATE
  Okay.

> *Beat.*

RUBY
  Night?

> *Beat.*

KATE
  Night.

> *Lights out.* KATE *is gone.*
>
> RUBY *is alone in the dark; she clearly doesn't like the dark. She turns on her phone flashlight, then finds a bathroom light to turn on. She sits for a minute and takes a breath.*
>
> *Then she gets undressed, back into "bed," then back out and gets her water bottle from her bag and a piece of gum. She settles*

herself back into "bed" and lies down, eyes open a couple minutes, with herself.

After a long moment, RUBY *gets up, moves toward where* KATE *has gone. Looks at the door* KATE *left through. Knocks on it.*

KATE *sticks her head out.* RUBY, *in silence, invites* KATE *to sit beside her on the couch.* KATE, *in silence, takes the offer. Carefully, respectfully, they silently negotiate the move to sit beside each other on the couch: both looking out, semi-comfortable.*

Just as carefully, KATE *offers herself to* RUBY. RUBY *accepts and moves toward* KATE. *It's slow, silent, awkward. Perhaps* RUBY *flinches at her sister's touch.*

KATE *holds* RUBY, *stroking her head.*

Blackout.

THE END

ACKNOWLEDGMENTS

First, I want to thank Chris Abraham and Liisa Repo-Martell for their support and guidance and their faith in me and my work. I also wish to thank Hazel and Leo Martell-Abraham.

Thanks to Crow's Theatre, Nightwood Theatre, Thousand Islands Playhouse, and Tarragon Theatre for their willingness to stage my plays. Brendan Healy and Owais Lightwala provided me with invaluable dramaturgical support.

Thank you to the various artists who brought these texts to life in ways that surprised and delighted me. There are many people who made important contributions to the production of these plays, including Geneviève Trottier, Annie Clarke, Laurence and Judy Siegel, Martha Burns, and Colin Rivers.

Thank you to my friends and family who continue to make time in their busy lives for my writing. I particularly want to thank David Sklar, Sydney Haslam, David Bradford, Thom Nyhuus, Ellie Ellwand, Rachel Cairns, Megan Robinson, Rose Tuong, Caitlin Murphy, Maggie Gray, Megan Wight, Richard Moon, Tess Degenstein, Deb Houston, Rob Kempson, Tanya Rintoul, Tom Strutt, and Brefny Caribou.

Finally, I want to express my gratitude to Diana Bentley, Kristin Booth, Trish Fagan, and Hannah Miller for their courage.

Ellie Moon is an actor and writer. She has acted in stage productions in both the UK and Canada, including with Soulpepper and the Segal Centre, among many others. Ellie's playwrighting debut, *Asking for It*, premiered as both Crow's and Nightwood's 2017–2018 season opener. Her second play, *What I Call Her*, premiered at Crow's the following year. Ellie's third play, *This Was the World*, premiered at Tarragon Theatre, where Ellie is currently playwright-in-residence, in their 2019–2020 season.

Photo: Bradley Golding